M000087189

The PSYCHOLOGY OF SALES SUCCESS

Learn to Think Like Your Customer to Close Every Sale

GERHARD GSCHWANDTNER
Founder and Publisher of *Selling Power*

McGRAW-HILL

NEW YORK | CHICAGO | SAN FRANCISCO | LISBON
LONDON | MADRID | MEXICO CITY | MILAN | NEW DELHI
SAN JUAN | SEOUL | SINGAPORE | SYDNEY | TORONTO

The McGraw·Hill Companies

Copyright © 2007 by Gerhard Gshwandtner. All rights reserved. Printed in the United States of America. Except as permitted under the United States Copyright Act of 1976, no part of this publication may be reproduced or distributed in any form or by any means, or stored in a database or retrieval system, without the prior written permission of the publisher.

1 2 3 4 5 6 7 8 9 0 DOC/DOC 0 9 8 7

ISBN-13: 978-0-07-147600-3
ISBN-10:   0-07-147600-8

McGraw-Hill books are available at special quantity discounts to use as premiums and sales promotions, or for use in corporate training programs. For more information, please write to the Director of Special Sales, Professional Publishing, McGraw-Hill, Two Penn Plaza, New York, NY 10121-2298. Or contact your local bookstore.

The publisher wishes to thank the following people for their participation in this book: All the experts in the field of sales and psychology who contributed their professional experience and thoughts, the editorial staff at *Selling Power* magazine, including L.B. Gschwandtner, Dana Ray, and Laurie Ross, art director Marc Oxborrow, and production manager Jeff Macharyas.

Library of Congress Cataloging-in-Publication Data

Gschwandtner, Gerhard.
   The psychology of sales success / by Gerhard Gschwandtner.
      p. cm.
   ISBN 0-07-147600-8 (alk. paper)
      1. Selling—Psychological aspects. 2. Success in business—Psychological aspects. I. Title.

HF5438.8.P75G793 2006
658.8501'9—dc22   2006046729

Contents

The PSYCHOLOGY OF SALES SUCCESS

PART I

UNDERSTANDING SUCCESS

Chapter 1

Attitude: Your Golden Opportunity for Success

Objective:

To explain the major difference a positive attitude can make in helping you become more successful in both your professional and private lives.

Synopsis:

1. Attitude dramatically affects outcomes.

2. A positive attitude can improve job performance, help overcome illness, and increase the pace with which people achieve goals.

3. Attitude comes in three forms: Persistence, where you interpret the customer's "no" as "tell me more"; Enthusiasm, which creates good feelings in your prospects about you and your product; and Value, when you show the customers the value of your company, your existing customers, your appearance, and your problem-solving creativity.

Attitude is a word with many meanings. To a market researcher it is a preference toward a product or a company; to a psychologist it is the cause of a particular behavior; to a salesperson it can often mean the difference between a sale closed or a sale lost. The best definition of a positive attitude I ever heard comes from a little-known story Zig Ziglar used to tell years ago. He had just come home from a series of seminars and was quite excited about the trip. When his wife picked him up at the airport, she took their daughter Susan and her friend along for the ride.

As Zig shared his excitement about the seminars with his wife, he overheard the following conversation from the back of the car: "What does your daddy do?" Zig's daughter, Susan, who was 10 years old at the time, answered, "Oh, that positive thinking stuff." Pause. "What is positive thinking?" Another pause. "Oh, you know, that's what makes you feel real good, even when you feel real bad." This little story raises an interesting question. If 10-year-olds know that positive thinking can change the way we feel by improving our feelings and attitudes, why is it that so few adults use it?

IMPACT OF ATTITUDES ON PERFORMANCE

According to Thomas J. Watson Sr., who managed his fledgling IBM Corporation on a philosophy of organizational spirit over material wealth, "The basic philosophy, spirit, and drive of an organization have far more to do with its relative achievements than do technological or economic resources."

Backing up that theory, a number of studies suggest that attitudes have a much more significant impact on job performance than most people suspect. Decades ago, Harvard University pioneered one of the first studies on the influence of attitudes on job security. Researchers measured the careers of 4,375 people who had lost their jobs because they failed to perform their duties to their employers' satisfaction. The study concluded that only one-third failed because of a lack of knowledge or skills, while a staggering two-thirds failed because of attitude problems alone.

Studies by Dr. Martin Seligman, a noted psychologist at the University of Pennsylvania, indicate that attitudes influence both job turnover and sales commissions.

Dr. Seligman studied the entire sales force of the Pennsylvania region of the Metropolitan Life Insurance Company. The research report, originally published in the *Journal of Personality and Social Psychology*, explains that the way in which agents explained their failures to make a sale made the difference between their becoming top sales achievers or quitting the company. "Individuals with a vulnerable explanatory style (i.e., the way a person explains an event; the particular slant he or she gives to the facts) will tend to explain the cause of their failure as more internal (I'm a loser); stable (I will never do anything right); and global (I never will succeed)," reported Seligman. "They will therefore blame themselves and expect failure to recur over a longer period of time and in more situations. Consequently, they will suffer more self-esteem deficits." In insurance sales, this translates into fewer sales attempts, less persistence, and, ultimately, quitting altogether.

The study concludes that those salespeople who had a more optimistic outlook sold 37 percent more insurance in their first year than did those with a pessimistic view. In addition, those with a positive explanatory style were twice as likely as those with a negative style to be among the agents still on the job.

The research appears to be another confirmation of the old saying, "It is our attitude and not our aptitude that determines our altitude."

ATTITUDES AND HEALTH

Dr. Christopher Peterson, associate professor of psychology at the University of Michigan, found that a confirmed pessimist is twice as likely to experience minor illnesses—the flu or a sore throat, for instance—as an unabashed optimist. Dr. Peterson noted that pessimists tend to abuse their bodies more; they smoke more, drink more, and get less sleep than optimists.

Every Day, in Every Way . . .

In 1922, Dr. Emile Coué, a pharmacist who lived in a small brick house in Nancy, France, became world famous. He had stumbled on a remarkable cure for a variety of ills—a cure which became known as the science of autosuggestion.

News reports from that time marveled, "Week after week, people stricken with disease come to Dr. Coué and go away strengthened, on the road to recovery, sometimes instantaneously cured."

The fame of Dr. Coué's achievements spread throughout the world. Thousands of people began to repeat his formula for health and happiness. Coué's technique was deceptively simple and his honesty quite disarming. "I have never cured anyone," he told reporters. "You can train your subconscious to radiate health and success."

What was Dr. Coué's attitude-building technique? "Every morning, before getting up, and every evening as soon as you are in bed, shut your eyes and repeat 20 times in succession, moving your lips (that is indispensable) and recounting mechanically, the following phrase: 'Day by day, in every way, I am getting better and better.'"

This sentence is so simple that its very simplicity makes it work. "In every way" broadcasts to our subconscious that we are getting better physically, mentally, professionally, financially, and any other way we can possibly imagine. "I am getting better" regenerates our hopes for the future. I may be improved tomorrow, but the next day there will be greater and greater improvement.

Why the lips moving? Because Coué suggested that the belief in the power of autosuggestion must come from the imagination, not the will. "Whenever the imagination and the will are in conflict, the imagination wins. The mechanical counting and the movement of the lips occupy the conscious mind, including the will, and leave the subconscious mind open to create positive images."

To illustrate that imagination is stronger than willpower, Dr. Coué asked people to imagine the following experiment. "Take a 30-foot plank, 1 foot wide, and put it on the ground. Walk across the entire length of the plank. Next, place the same plank between two large buildings, 150 feet above the ground. Then step on the same plank and walk across to the other building. Chances are that you would not walk on that high plank."

Does Dr. Coué's autosuggestion work? Try it. If Dr. Coué were alive today he would tell you what he once told a reporter: "To become master of oneself, it is enough to think that one is becoming so. It is not in me but in yourself that you must have confidence, for it is in yourself alone that dwells the force which can make you the master. My part simply consists of teaching you to make use of that force."

THE RIGHT BUSINESS ATTITUDE

The secrets to a successful business attitude are all contained within the small word "business." When we separate the word into its component letters B-U-S-I-N-E-S-S, we find four surprising secrets:

"U" and "I" are in it. Without "U" and "I" there would be no business.

The "U" comes before the "I," which means that "U" have priority. It's simply good business to put the customer first.

The "I" is silent. This reminds us not to talk ourselves out of a sale. If we want to be successful in business, we need to master the fine art of shutting up and tuning in to our customer's needs.

The "U" is pronounced like an "I." This is the biggest secret of good business and good selling. We always should strive to see the "U" from the "I" perspective. This means that to succeed in business, we need to walk the extra mile in our customer's shoes.

Another researcher, Dr. Winston Parris of Vanderbilt University, studied women undergoing minor surgery. Women with positive attitudes were less likely to experience minor postoperative pain, nausea, vomiting, and other complications requiring an overnight hospital stay.

Schering-Plough's Research Institute of Molecular Biology in Palo Alto, California, reported that a team of scientists found a link between brain activity and the activity of lymphocytes (the white blood cells that defend against invasion), suggesting that a good mental attitude can help the body fight off disease. In another study involving 69 women who had breast cancer, the women were asked how they viewed the nature and seriousness of the disease. Seventy-five percent of the women who had reacted to the disease with a fighting spirit survived and had no recurrence of the cancer. Only 35 percent of the women who had accepted the disease with a feeling of helplessness were still alive with no recurrence. The study appears to suggest that our attitudes decide whether we are part of the cure or part of the illness.

How can we develop new and better attitudes that lead to better health, higher income, more secure employment, higher career satisfaction, and a greater level of success? The answer is simple: one attitude at a time. It appears the more accurate we are in pinpointing our attitude needs, the easier it becomes for us to build more productive attitudes. Like a building begins with a foundation, the foundation for a new attitude is awareness.

The following Attitude Awareness Quiz has been developed to help you pinpoint your current attitude-building needs.

YOUR PERSONAL ATTITUDE CHECKUP

Please circle yes or no for each question and date your questionnaire. As you will see, every "No" reply represents an opportunity for changing your attitude. Look up the solutions following the quiz, and work on your attitude for one week. Repeat the attitude checkup every week until you can answer all questions with a "Yes!"

1. Is my current mood free of negative experiences from the past?
   Yes   *No*

2. Is my current mood hopeful and optimistic in anticipation of the future?
   Yes   *No*

3. Do I currently feel that I am in control of my life?
   Yes   *No*

4. Do I feel that the problems I face are really stimulating challenges?
   Yes   *No*

5. Do I feel free from self-abuse such as overeating, drinking, or drugs?
   Yes   *No*

6. Do I currently pursue a written, realistic, and challenging goal?
   Yes   *No*

7. Am I committed to an ongoing exercise program?
   Yes   *No*

8. Are my family relationships a source of love, pride, and support?
   Yes   *No*

9. Do I consider myself a success?
   Yes   *No*

10. Are my thoughts stimulated by speakers, writers, and personal heroes?
    Yes   *No*

11. Do I seek out challenges that are in line with my present potential?
    Yes   *No*

12. Do I automatically look for the positive in every situation?
    Yes   *No*

Please review the following attitude recovery steps to improve your attitude scores the next time you take this test a week from today.

HOW DO YOU WRITE THE WORD "ATTITUDE"?

Attitude trainer Rich Wilkins asks his students to write the word "Attitude" on a piece of paper with their right hand. (Lefthanded people need to write with their left hand first.) Then he asks his students to switch hands, write the same word again, and judge their handwriting. Course participants usually say, "That's terrible," or "simply awful." Wilkins continues with a smile, "When you look at the word 'Attitude' written by the hand you are not familiar with, you see a picture of the kind of attitude we usually have when we are trying to do something new."

HOW TO BUILD A POSITIVE ATTITUDE

Unfinished business tends to be remembered longer. Learn how to bring your negative experiences to an earlier "close." Some of the best techniques for managing moods have been described by Dr. David Burns in his book *Feeling Good*. Dr. Burns suggests writing automatic thoughts following a negative experience on the left-hand side of a piece of paper and then objectively appraising each thought one by one with a rational response.

James Baldwin wrote, "Not everything that is faced can be changed, but nothing can be changed until it is faced." Facing reality takes a lot of courage, but once we accept what is (and let go of the illusions of what "is not"), hope begins to grow. If you've lost hope following a setback and you get stuck in "low" for an extended period of time, seek professional help.

Many people want to change the world to improve their lives. What a wasted effort. If they would only improve themselves, they would be better off and so would the world. Begin your self-improvement process with moderate, but regular, physical exercise. If you already exercise, start a new hobby, enroll in a Yoga class, and relearn to look at life one day at a time.

Positive thinkers don't eliminate negative words from their vocabularies; they only change their definitions. Define problems as wake-up calls for creativity, as the diamond dust with which nature polishes its jewels, as temporary inconveniences. Remember Dr. Norman Vincent Peale's words, "The only people without problems I have ever known are in the cemetery." Reread his best seller, *The Power of Positive Thinking*.

When life deals you a bad hand, don't get mad at the cards, but reshuffle the deck. Self-abuse is a form of depression. Read the book *Feeling Good* by Dr. David Burns.

In 1952, 3 percent of the graduating class of Yale University responded "yes" to a survey asking them if they had written goals. Twenty years later, the net worth of those 3 percent who had written goals was greater than the combined net worth of the other 97 percent of their graduating class. Remember: goals pay. Remember: goals are dreams with a deadline.

Dr. Wayne Dyer jogs eight miles every day. Zig Ziglar has been an enthusiastic runner for many years. Dr. Denis Waitley powerwalks. A Gallup survey claims that among the men and women who have taken up exercise recently, 62 percent report a new surge of energy, 37 percent a rise in creativity on the job, 46 percent more confidence and self-respect, 51 percent better looks, 45 percent better love life, 55 percent less stress, 44 percent greater job satisfaction, and 66 percent a more relaxed life. Great evidence for action. Get going.

Mary Kay Ash, who founded Mary Kay Cosmetics, encouraged her salespeople to establish simple priorities in their lives: "God first, family second, work third." Mo Siegel, the founder of Celestial Seasonings, once said, "Of all the great achievements, the raising of a good family is the greatest achievement. You could build any size corporation imaginable, and it would not equal the success of raising good children. That's the highest task a person could do in life."

Yes, we are all a success in the making. Success is not a destination, but a journey. You can begin your journey any time you choose.

Fred Smith, a management consultant, once said, "Change your heroes and you will change the direction of your life." Read the biographies of successful people like Benjamin Franklin, Abraham Lincoln, Thomas Edison, Walter Chrysler, Henry Ford, Eleanor Roosevelt, Helen Keller, Mary Kay Ash, Albert Einstein, and Madame Curie, and capture the spirit of greatness. There are more inspiring biographies of successful people in the average bookstore than you can read in one year.

If you don't, you will soon hear yourself complain, "Life has become much tougher than it used to be." Zig Ziglar writes, "The tougher we are on ourselves, the easier life becomes; the easier we are on ourselves, the tougher life becomes." Always seek out challenges that are slightly beyond your grasp. Never aim at repeating your past performance. Aim at improving your best performance.

Positive thinkers don't limit their vision to reality. They always see reality plus the possibility of what can happen through the power of positive imagination. God gave us two eyes, and we can use them when they are open and when they are closed. When they are open, we see reality; when they are closed, we can see anything we want to. Close your eyes and choose to see the positive that is within all of us.

ACTION STEPS

ATTITUDE

1. Since you can't control life, manage your moods instead.
2. Dispense with self-blame, turn problems into challenges, set accomplishable goals, and build your hope for the future.
3. Establish priorities. Families and health should always take precedence over business.
4. Keep the challenges coming. Expand your vision to encompass the ever-growing possibilities in life.

Chapter 2

Achievement Factors: A Study of Superachievers

Objective:

To describe the unifying factors that separate top achievers from average achievers and how you can increase the likelihood that you will achieve top performance.

Synopsis:

1. Superachievers and Average Achievers reached similar levels of education, yet Superachievers by far exceed Average Achievers in income and life satisfaction.

2. Superachievers enjoy better health and are significantly more satisfied with their health than average achievers.

3. Superachievers follow thought patterns that are clearly distinct from the thought patterns of average achievers. While Superachievers think more constructively, Average Achievers show more self-defeating thought patterns.

4. Superachievers are more skilled at learning from their own experiences and the experiences of their role models and mentors. They accept the challenges involved in growing as necessary and inevitable.

5. Superachievers show greater social navigation skills and experience fewer psychosomatic symptoms. Their explanatory styles are more constructive, positive, and optimistic.

Ihrough my position as publisher of *Selling Power*, I have had the opportunity to interview many Superachievers. These men and women share some common characteristics. Most came from modest backgrounds and rose to higher levels of success than other members of their families, contemporaries, or friends. All became wealthy, influential, respected, and, as a group, more satisfied with work, marriage, and their lives in general. The majority of these Superachievers became successful business executives, while others became leading figures in the fields of entertainment, medicine, sports, education, and science.

As I met these Superachievers and observed them in social gatherings, I wondered why so many radiate a special quality that almost defies description. In their presence, people tend to feel differently about themselves. In addition, the Superachievers seem to draw the best out of others. All the Superachievers have reached superior economic wealth ranging from several million dollars up to $500 million.

Although many Superachievers have discussed the "secrets" of their success, and although many of their actions have been described in great detail, very little is known about thought processes Superachievers use to reach very high levels of success.

Equally little is known about what Average Achievers can do to reach the kind of success attained by Superachievers. To gain more insight into these questions, *Selling Power* asked Dr. Seymour Epstein, a noted psychologist known for his research on constructive thinking and life success, to conduct a scientific study to identify the most striking differences between a group of 50 Superachievers and a group of 200 sales and marketing executives (called Average Achievers throughout this report). Given the fact that it took about one hour to complete all survey questions, the final response rate of 52.5 percent was extraordinary.

PERSONAL DIFFERENCES BETWEEN SUPERACHIEVERS (SAs) AND AVERAGE ACHIEVERS (AAs)

1. Educational background:

Similarities: It was interesting to note that the parents of both groups, Superachievers and Average Achievers, reached similar levels of education. It was even more interesting that both groups far exceeded their parents' level of education.

Differences: Superachievers performed significantly better in high school than Average Achievers.

2. Business attitudes:

Similarities: Superachievers and Average Achievers believe that to be successful in business, it is important to be a warm and cooperative person. Both groups are equally aggressive in business and about life in general.

Differences: In their business interactions, Superachievers appear to be more sensitive to other people's needs.

3. Age:

	SAs	AAs
Under 30 years	0%	13%
30–40 years	16	38
40–50 years	16	37
50–60 years	36	10
Over 60 years	32	02

4. Physical activity and recreation:

Similarities: Both groups spend 3–6 hours a week on passive recreation such as watching movies or TV or attending sports events. They tend to spend an equal amount of time on physical exercise.

Differences: Superachievers pay a little closer attention to diet than Average Achievers. In addition, Superachievers tend to take more vacations away from home.

5. Marital status:

	%SAs	%AAs
Single, never married	4	8
Single, divorced, or separated	0	9
Single, widowed	8	0
Divorced and remarried	40	16
Married, never divorced	48	67

LESSONS ON ACHIEVEMENT FACTORS

1. Superachievers are less naive, categorical, and superstitious and are more action-oriented in their thinking.
2. Superachievers are optimistic about the future but also make specific plans to realize their optimistic dreams.
3. Superachievers find role models to help them blueprint future success.
4. Superachievers handle failure and disappointment better than Average Achievers. They know that failures are essential before success is achieved.
5. Superachievers work hard, but they also work smart. They know how to manage their available resources for the maximum impact.

HOW SUCCESSFUL ARE SUPERACHIEVERS?

1. Financial success: Superachievers are wealthier.

It is important to note that the economic status of the Superachievers surveyed was slightly lower during their childhood years than the economic status of Average Achievers during the same time period. Although both groups enjoy a much higher economic status today, the Superachiever group has clearly achieved a dramatic increase in financial success. In addition, Superachievers enjoy greater levels of satisfaction with their income.

2. Family success: Superachievers enjoy their families more.

Similarities: Both groups surveyed put a high priority on family life. Superachievers and Average Achievers enjoy an equally close relationship with their children.

Differences: Superachievers tend to be slightly more satisfied with their marriages and more satisfied with their family lives. Superachievers also spend significantly more time with their spouses or children as compared to Average Achievers.

3. Life success: Superachievers find more meaning in life.

Similarities: Both groups feel that material possessions are only moderately important in life.

Differences: Superachievers are far more satisfied with life in general than are Average Achievers. They also feel that they are fulfilling their potential in life. When asked about their sense of contribution, Superachievers clearly showed a greater feeling of satisfaction with their ability to contribute something of value to others.

4. Work success: Superachievers work more effectively.

Similarities: Superachievers and Average Achievers seem to work equally hard at their occupations, with an average work week of slightly over 50 hours.

Differences: It is not surprising that Superachievers advance in their jobs significantly faster than Average Achievers. The responses also indicate that Superachievers find significantly higher levels of satisfaction with their work and clearly express superior levels of satisfaction in what they accomplish.

5. Social success: Superachievers have better social skills.

Similarities: Among the many categories compared in the study, in the category of social success and satisfaction, Superachievers are clearly a breed apart. There are few similarities in this category— mainly significant differences as listed below.

Differences: Superachievers appear to possess the kind of interpersonal skills that everyone else is looking for. As a result, Superachievers exceed Average Achievers in popularity. When a Superachiever speaks in a group setting, he or she will have far more influence on the group than an Average Achiever. In general, other people view a Superachiever's level of success as far superior compared to that of the Average Achiever. On a more personal level, Superachievers tend to have a greater ability to make friends and feel more satisfied with their established circle of friends. Superachievers also have a significantly higher number of trusted friends compared to Average Achievers.

DIFFERENCES IN PHYSICAL AND PSYCHOLOGICAL HEALTH

1. Physical health: Superachievers enjoy better health.

Similarities: In many categories, Superachievers and Average Achievers reported very similar health data like blood pressure, frequency of respiratory infections, or limited use of alcohol or drugs.

Minor differences: Superachievers have a tendency to sleep better, to have fewer minor illnesses, and to experience fewer accidents due to carelessness. In general, Superachievers tend to have a smaller number of ailments compared to Average Achievers.

Major differences: Although the average age of the Superachievers surveyed is higher than the Average Achievers, Superachievers are significantly more satisfied with their health.

2. Psychological health: Superachievers feel better.

Similarities: Superachievers and Average Achievers very rarely require psychological counseling.

Minor differences: Average Achievers tend to experience slightly higher amounts of anxiety. They also tend to have more sleeping problems than Superachievers. When asked about how frequently they experience feelings of depression, Average Achievers reported a slightly higher number.

Major differences: Superachievers have significantly fewer problems with managing anger compared to Average Achievers. Superachievers experience significantly fewer psychosomatic symptoms. When asked about how frequently they experience "a warm glow of serenity or good feelings, or feeling exhilarated and on top of the world," Superachievers reported significantly higher frequency rates than Average Achievers.

HOW DO SUPERACHIEVERS THINK DIFFERENTLY TO ACHIEVE HIGHER LEVELS OF SUCCESS?

To determine how Superachievers think differently, and to clarify the relationship between thinking and success, Dr. Seymour Epstein's "Constructive Thinking Inventory" test was given to all participants. This test has been validated through extensive research, and some of the findings have been reported in psychological journals, as well as *The New York Times*. For many decades, educators have assumed that academically correct thinking would lead to success in life. However, recent research suggests that IQ is not strongly associated with success in life. Dr. Epstein stated in an article for *The New York Times*: "Intellectual gifts don't mean that you will earn the most money or achieve the most recognition in life."

Constructive Thinking Inventory—A Sample Question

For the following statements, answer "definitely false," "mostly false," "undecided," "mostly true," or "definitely true."

THE EXPERIENTIAL MIND VS. THE RATIONAL MIND

Dr. Epstein's research seems to indicate that there are two minds: the experiential mind and the rational mind. The first, the experiential, is shaped by experiences. The second, the rational, is shaped by education. The experiential mind makes instant decisions, while the rational mind follows the path of reason. The experiential mind controls how we react to the world emotionally. The rational mind controls how well we do verbally or mathematically.

The performance of the experiential mind can be measured with the Constructive Thinking Inventory, while the performance of the rational mind is traditionally measured by IQ tests. The experiential mind expands and grows through new experiences. The rational mind expands and grows through study and reasoning. The experiential mind is directly related to success in all aspects of life. The rational mind is more strongly associated with success in school and in solving abstract problems.

1. I am the kind of person who takes action rather than just thinks or complains about a situation.
2. I don't let little things bother me.
3. I tend to take things personally.
4. I get so distressed when I notice that I am doing poorly in something that it makes me do worse.

The Superachiever answers for this test sample would be:

1. Definitely true
2. Definitely true

3. Definitely false
4. Definitely false

Based on such questions, Dr. Epstein was able to identify nine different forms of constructive thinking in which Superachievers clearly outperform Average Achievers. Below is a listing of those thought patterns with the most significant difference to Average Achievers' thoughts in the first place, and the type of thinking with the least significant differences in last place.

THOUGHTS ABOUT THINKING

As one thinketh in his heart, so is he.

King Solomon

The mind is everything; what you think, you become.

Gautama Buddha

Sooner or later you act out what you really think.

Japanese proverb

Great men are those who see that thoughts rule the world.

Ralph Waldo Emerson

No one deceives us more than our own thoughts.

Silesian proverb

There is nothing either good or bad except that thinking makes it so.

William Shakespeare

The wise man never says "I did not think."

Spanish proverb

Speaking without thinking is like shooting without taking aim.

Anonymous

He who thinks far, goes far.

Belgian proverb

1. **Capacity for coping with disapproval.** Superachievers think in ways that make them far less sensitive to disapproval and rejection. They brush off rejection more quickly, they don't get as upset by it, and they don't worry as much about what other people think of them. When being made fun of, Superachievers are less sensitive than Average Achievers.

2. **More action-oriented thinking.** Superachievers think in ways that facilitate effective action. They don't spend a lot of time worrying about a deadline; instead, they go ahead and do the work. When a large amount of work piles up, Superachievers are not afraid of trying hard and failing. If they make a mistake, they take action immediately and quickly recover from their mistakes.

3. **Effective thoughts to cope with negative emotions.** Superachievers' thoughts are more focused on the task at hand. They refuse to let their minds drift to unpleasant events of the past. They don't let little things bother them. If they can't do anything about a negative situation, they don't worry about it, and they move on with their lives. They don't dwell on their mistakes, but they learn what they can from them and then move on to other events. If something unpleasant should happen to them, they isolate the experience and don't overgeneralize about all the things wrong in their lives.

4. **Less superstitious thinking.** Superachievers' actions are less handicapped by superstitious thoughts. When something good is happening to them, they don't think it will automatically be balanced with something bad. They don't give up hope in view of the possibility that what they hope for might not happen. When something bad happens, they don't assume that more bad things are likely to follow. They refuse to think that their thoughts about success can actually prevent them from succeeding. Superachievers don't believe in good or bad omens.

5. **Better thought for coping with failure.** Superachievers don't think that they are failures if they don't achieve their goals.

If they fail, they don't take failure very hard. Their thoughts neutralize perfectionistic impulses effectively; they don't tell themselves, "Unless I do a perfect job, I am a failure." Superachievers view failures as an important part of learning and refuse to equate failure with low self-worth. Their correct thinking saves them from psychological pain. If they fail, Superachievers don't invest too much time worrying about it, but learn from the experience and move on. As a result they are able to take reasonable risks and maintain a high level of productivity.

6. **Less categorical thinking.** Superachievers don't restrict their thinking by establishing rigid patterns. They don't classify people as "for" or "against" them, and they don't divide others into "winners" and "losers"; they accept people for who they are as individuals. They don't believe that when people treat them badly, they should retaliate the same way. They are flexible in their business dealings and favor compromise over rigid decisions. They refuse to see the world as "black and white," and they don't think that there is only one right answer to every question. They allow themselves to trust others, and they accept people as they are without judging them.

7. **Absence of naive optimism.** Superachievers think thoughts through without jumping to false conclusions. They don't conclude from a single success experience that they will always do a good job at everything. When something good happens to them, they don't believe that more good things will automatically follow. When they are loved by someone, they don't conclude that they will be able to accomplish whatever they want to. If they do well on an important task, they don't believe that they are a total success. Superachievers are able to see their actions and the world in a healthy, realistic perspective. They are optimists, yet realists.

8. **High on optimism and planning.** Superachievers think optimistically and plan purposefully. When they have to do unpleasant chores, they make the best of it by thinking pleasant

thoughts. They look at challenges not as things to fear, but as opportunities to test themselves and to learn. They think encouraging thoughts in the face of difficulty and easily find ways to look at the positive side of life. Superachievers get important tasks done quickly by establishing clear priorities and developing an effective action plan. Once the plan is established, they stick to it. They carefully think through future events in advance and imagine the best outcome.

9. **Low levels of esoteric thinking.** Superachievers don't waste their time in unproductive thoughts or fanciful musing. They don't worry whether other people are able to read thoughts, they don't pay too much attention to astrology, they don't think that terrible thoughts about a person can affect that person, they don't believe that the moon or the stars can affect people's thinking, and they ignore tales about ghosts and have little interest in good-luck charms, crystals, rabbits' feet, flying saucers, palm readers, and fortune tellers. Superachievers think constructively and, as a result, act constructively. Their levels of thinking determine their levels of success.

HOW TO THINK LIKE A SUPERACHIEVER

The kind of thoughts that lead to success levels similar to those of the Superachievers described in this survey are predominately shaped by the experiential mind. Although these thoughts can be understood by everyone through book learning, they can't be translated into action skills through study, only through experiences. Since our thoughts lead us to experiences that are consistent with our thinking, the first step to new learning begins with seeking out experiences that stimulate new ways of thinking and better ways of functioning.

Superachievers tend to embrace new experiences more eagerly than Average Achievers; they leave their comfort zones more willingly and, as a result, become more familiar with the process of growing than others do. They also view the anxiety or pain involved in new challenges as a small price to pay compared to the new levels of success they enjoy in return. Superachiever thinking can be learned; however, the process takes time, patience, skillful mentoring, and persistence. Below are five suggestions for seeking out the kind of experiences that lead to Superachiever thinking.

1. **Find role models or mentors to help you grow.** Become more assertive in seeking advice from higher-level people than you are used to. Superachievers tend to find the best available mentors throughout all stages of life. They value their own growth too much to be deterred by fears of possible rejection. There are many more people in high places willing to give advice than there are people actively seeking advice.

2. **Don't "should" at yourself—remove the psychological bullets from your vocabulary.** To practice a new way of thinking, begin by practicing a new way of talking to yourself. Superachievers develop the capacity to put their thoughts into a psychologically helpful, rather than harmful, perspective. For example, when faced with a negative situation, they may respond with "Oh, that's inconvenient" instead of personalizing the situation by blaming themselves for falling short like "I should have done a better job" or "I should be doing much better."

3. **Increase your mental "navigation" skills.** Superachievers navigate through mental, social, or organizational mazes with astonishing ease. They respond to situations in more effective ways than Average Achievers. One of the keys to increasing mental navigation skills is to use imagination as an experiential form of thinking. Begin imagining new possibilities, new ways of acting, new ways of overcoming obstacles or roadblocks. It is important that we use imagination constructively so it will enhance our ability to deal with situations. However, if we overinvest in fantasy, it can turn against us. When things don't

turn out the way we imagined, it is good to remember that we're just dealing with mental possibilities, not with reality. Imagination and fantasy are mental games. As with any game, we can assign a value to the bets we place on the outcome. Superachievers handle emotional investments in fantasy more carefully than Average Achievers. Superachievers invest Monopoly money where Average Achievers use real currency. Harnessing the powers of the imagination begins with avoiding heavy betting on the outcome of our dreams. It is the best protection against suffering disappointment.

4. **Test the realities of your thinking.** Superachievers play mental detective, constantly searching for clues and evidence leading to reality. The less we think in rigid categories, the easier it is for us to perceive opportunities; the less we harbor superstitious thoughts, the better we can prepare and plan our future; the fewer naive thoughts we allow to cloud our judgment, the more effectively we begin to function.

   Average Achievers are often unable to put things in perspective because their protective and unrealistic thoughts stand in the way of seeing things objectively.

5. **Face difficulties and enjoy growth.** Accept the fact that in order to grow, we must face difficult experiences. Superachievers accept the challenges of growing as necessary and inevitable. They know intuitively how their experiential mind works and seek out the experiences that enhance their growth. Yet they are not afraid to say no to challenges that are beyond their capabilities to handle.

ACTION STEPS

ACHIEVEMENT FACTORS

1. Follow your intuition to discover the right application for our abilities.
2. Find role models to emulate.
3. Look forward to and embrace change—it is the key to growth and success.
4. Don't be your worst critic. Why not be your number one cheerleader instead?
5. Constantly push the limits of your abilities.

Chapter 3

Concentration: The Key to Selling Power

Objective:

To provide you with effective tools to eliminate distractions and increase your ability to focus on pressing tasks at hand.

Synopsis:

1. Stress can derail even the most carefully prepared sales presentations by affecting your concentration.
2. Interruptions by others can be avoided; it is the internal interruptions that break up your concentration.
3. Many people interrupt their own concentration by mentally justifying procrastination and creating other mental roadblocks.

Have you ever found yourself saying, "I just can't concentrate on this job" or "I'll never be able to get this done"? Closing a sale often depends on how well you concentrate on the total situation. The ability to concentrate, to focus all your attention and energy on a single task or situation, comes easily when you are using it on something you find easy or have a strong desire to do. However, when it comes to something more difficult, like selling to a tough customer, you may find it hard to keep your concentration on track. There are several ways you can use the power of your mind to improve your concentration at critical times. Let's look at what interferes with concentration to learn how you can remove the roadblocks and improve your ability to concentrate.

The first obstacle to concentration is stress. Can you recall a sales presentation that went badly because you felt nervous and uptight, didn't make all the points you wanted to, or left an indifferent or poor impression on the potential customer? Were you worrying about your image, the tough reputation of your prospect, or an argument you had with your spouse that morning? These are the types of stress that can ruin your concentration.

At times like these, you can apply three mental techniques to help you concentrate: (1) the nature scene, (2) breathing out, and (3) the countdown. Each of these is used in meditation techniques taught by the Mind Power Institute.

THE NATURE SCENE

This technique is to close your eyes and bring to mind a beautiful, relaxing scene from nature . . . a mountain lake, ocean beach, or forest stream. Visualize the place in your mind's eye as if you were there. Review all its details. Is the sun shining? Is the breeze blowing? Is it warm or cool? Are there any sounds? The idea is to paint a vivid picture, so complete that it creates a placid, relaxed mood for you. Doing this for a minute or two can produce surprisingly relaxing results by focusing your mind and mentally detaching yourself from what you are doing on the physical, conscious level.

BREATHING OUT

The next technique is to close your eyes while you are in a comfortable position and pretend your breath is a pump you will use to

---

Expert Advice: This chapter features contributions from William Schwartz.

rid yourself of tension and replace it with relaxation. With each breath, tell yourself mentally you are breathing out tension and breathing in peace, relaxation, and confidence, and as you do this, focus your attention on the parts of your body, beginning at the top of your head. Mentally tell yourself that you are breathing out the tension in your scalp and breathing in relaxation, and that you can feel it becoming more and more relaxed. Do this first with your scalp, then on down to your forehead, the muscles around your eyes, your cheeks, jaws, neck, shoulders, and so on all the way down to your feet and toes. Spend time and focus your attention on each part as you go until you find yourself calm and refreshed.

THE COUNTDOWN

The third method is the countdown. In a comfortable position, close your eyes and focus your mental attention on the number 21. Repeat it mentally a number of times while visualizing it on a red background and telling yourself each time you are going deeper and deeper into a state of relaxation. Continue on with the number 20, 19, 18, and so on until you reach the number 1. When visualizing the numbers, see 21, 20, and 19 on a red background; 18, 17, and 16 on an orange background; 15, 14, and 13 on a yellow background; 12, 11, and 10 on a green background; 9, 8, and 7 on a blue background; 6, 5, and 4 on a purple background; and 3, 2, and 1 on a violet background. By the time you have finished, you should be much more relaxed, physically, mentally, and emotionally.

You can deal with stress using techniques like these while you prepare yourself for sales presentations, closings, and other situations. When a lack of concentration caused by stress makes you forgetful, insensitive to the prospect's needs or questions, appear to lack confidence in yourself or your product, or fail to follow through with promised information or action, then it's time to save the sale by getting rid of the stress!

The second roadblock to concentration is interruptions. These can play havoc with your concentration on important jobs.

Frustrating external interruptions can be dealt with. People, telephone calls, and the like can easily be cut off—either you or your prospect may ask for no interruptions. Your prospect may welcome that as much as you do, so suggest it with the message that you both can save time by focusing on his or her needs. If external interruptions cannot be avoided, try to arrange a different time and/or place to do business. This can relieve the pressure both you and your prospect may be feeling at the time.

Internal interruptions are the sneakier ones inside your own mind—sneakier because you may not always be aware of them, though they are just as damaging to your concentration as the external ones. They are mental attitudes or lack of mental discipline you can overcome with specific mental techniques. Let's look at some of these problems and the techniques for overcoming them.

Have you ever found yourself saying, "I just can't concentrate on this job" or "I'll never be able to get this done"? When you do this, you are programming yourself to have these statements come true—to make things more difficult or that deadline impossible to meet. Catch yourself when saying these things and instead say, "I am able to concentrate on this job" or "I will get this done on time and it will be successful." Since we can program ourselves with our words to act the way we do, whether consciously or not, try taking advantage of this power by using your mind to program positive mental traits that will help you, rather than hinder you.

The third roadblock to concentration is bad mental habits. Some salespeople mentally justify putting aside what needs to be done now. Look at how you do things now and the way you dealt with sales situations that turned out unsuccessfully in the past. You may find a negative pattern. Sometimes we get into negative daily routines that we find ways to justify. Concentration often deteriorates when we get distracted by these routines. We get the "easy stuff" done so we can convince ourselves that we accomplished something.

If you see yourself doing this, mentally prepare yourself to conquer these patterns—plan and prioritize tasks so that what needs to be done will be done when it should be.

Mental interruptions can be turned aside by using positive incentives on yourself. If you are tired, or you will be dealing with someone you do not like, or you have mental worries or physical problems (a headache, for example), try this: Pause and review the situation mentally, with your eyes closed, and identify the problem, then promise yourself some positive incentive if the obstacle will stop bothering you. Mentally tell yourself what good thing you will do for yourself—a hot tub, a day off, a night out—if your mind will not let these interruptions get to you. Just one thing: Always honor these promises, or your mind and body will ignore future promises for good behavior.

Here are a few ways to maintain concentration on your customer and his or her needs with other techniques.

Visualization. Our successes and our failures come equally from our thoughts, mental pictures, and attitudes. If we think, see, believe, and feel we will be successful at something, we will! If we think, see, believe, or feel doubtful about it, we won't! Before each sales situation, stop and close your eyes, seeing it in your mind as if it were a movie or a series of pictures. Visualize it ending with the results you want—a sale, a problem resolved, an objection over-come, a question answered, a happy customer, or a signed con-tract. We call this method "projecting." We project the thoughts of the pictured success out and away from us, allowing them to become true in reality.

One step at a time. Many sales situations are small campaigns of several days. It is always a good idea to plan ahead and anticipate what might happen. Keep your mind on each step—why worry about Step 12 when Step 1 is still in the works? Planning ahead is fine, but sometimes an early step might turn out differently than you anticipated. Later ones may have to be changed as well. Focus on one at a time to make sure each comes out with the desired result, or the next step might never happen!

Positive attitudes about your work. Good concentration is easier when you feel really motivated and excited about what you are doing. Mentally tell yourself often that you are offering the best product or service in the world, and that there are meaningful reasons for you to be selling it. The service you are performing for the benefit of others and the need you are filling are far more satisfying and exciting reasons for selling than just to "make a buck" or "put food on the table." Mentally convincing yourself—through visualization and repetition—of the excitement of the job produces the attitude that makes concentration—and success—much easier.

We have techniques to help concentration, by removing the barriers of stress, interruptions, and bad mental habits. Use the techniques outlined here and see for yourself that mind power can give you the concentration you need at any time and in any place to improve your selling power.

ACTION STEPS

CONCENTRATION

1. Develop exercises you can use when you identify breakdowns in your concentration.
2. When you find yourself using negative internal dialogue, identify it and turn those statements around to be supportive and concentration-building.
3. Bad mental habits can be turned aside with positive incentives. Make yourself promises of rewards if the obstacles will stop bothering you.
4. Don't get ahead of yourself; if you're on Step 1 in the selling process, don't concern yourself with Step 12.
5. Constantly improve your motivation and job excitement. It is much easier to stay focused when you are motivated and excited about what you are doing.

Chapter 4

Confidence: How to Master the Inner Game of Selling

Objective:

To help you address the negative influences on your selling confidence so you can achieve a level of accomplishment equal to your true abilities.

Synopsis:

1. Confidence is the key to moving beyond the numerous conflicting emotions involved in the selling field.
2. To succeed in selling, everyone must find the right way to achieve a level of balance.
3. Sales requires that you use both love and aggression to close sales. Finding harmony between the two can mean the difference between success and failure.
4. Being creative builds our overall confidence. Creativity is often lost in the shuffle of overhead projectors and other visual aids.

Art Mortell was an unhappy young man. Having convinced his employer to give him a chance at sales, Mortell had set out on his first day with the boundless energy of his 21 years. Two hours later, he had knocked on 19 doors and been turned down 19 times. Depressed and dejected, he trudged two miles back to his office, convinced he had no future in sales.

A couple of weeks later, Mortell accidentally came upon his notes from that miserable day. He was surprised to discover that two people had been interested enough to ask for samples. Mortell realized that he had been so discouraged by the 17 negative responses, he had failed to notice any success. The rest, as they say, is history. Mortell delivered the samples and made one sale. Within two years, he was working for IBM and enjoying a fruitful selling career.

Nearly 30 years later, Arthur Mortell became one of the leading motivational speakers in the country. His clients include former employer IBM, and Shearson Lehman, Merrill Lynch, and Smith Barney, to name a few.

From his first experience in sales, he learned that the ability to succeed is closely connected to the ability to handle failure. To understand how to obtain the self-confidence you need for success, I asked Mortell to share his views on how to achieve sales success and how to have more fun while you're doing it.

"You know, from childhood we are conditioned to feel successful only if we succeed most of the time," says Mortell. "If we get 19 right out of 20 on a test, then we get positive feedback. In selling, however, the ratios are the other way around. People are often rude to us. We confront resistance. We get 19 wrong out of 20, or 95 negatives out of 100. We call 100 people, and only 5 may be receptive and only one person may buy, and it's very discouraging. And yet, people realize as they grow up that they need to change their attitudes toward negative experiences. It's a matter of percentages. The ratio has changed.

"The idea of feeling successful in an environment in which failure and rejection are normal indicates that failure and rejection may have trade-offs and benefits after all. In fact, that's one of my major theses—that failure is only an experience that was less than what we expected. If we can somehow change our expectations, our percep-tions and our reactions, our feelings will start changing.

Expert Advice: This chapter features contributions from Elaine Evans.

TIPS

8 ADDITIONAL TIPS FOR BUILDING CONFIDENCE

1 Don't be timid. This means letting customers know your time is valuable. Instead of saying, "Thank you for your time," say, "Enjoyed our visit" or "It was nice to get together."

2 This also holds for follow-up letters. Don't say, "Thank you for taking time out of your busy schedule." Instead try, "Glad we could get together."

3 Limit the length of time you will wait for a customer to see you to 15 minutes. If you willingly wait 30–45 minutes or longer, the message you send—"Your time is valuable while my time is meaningless"—is clear. After 15 minutes, tell the receptionist that this is obviously a bad time, and if the customer can't see you now, you would prefer to reschedule and come back another time.

4 Use role-playing, repetition, and videotaping of sales calls to eliminate all aspects of timidity from your selling style.

5 Understand that when you sell, you are doing things for people, not to them.

6 Always work on your product knowledge, responses to objections, and other confidence builders.

7 Instead of concentrating on all the factors that could potentially keep you from closing sales, try instead focusing on your customers and all the factors you can work on to cause them to buy.

8 Make sure you are selling for the right reasons. Stay focused on your goal. Confidence builds as you achieve small steps to your big dreams.

"Back in 1961 as a beginning salesperson, I learned a valuable lesson—not to let rejection overwhelm me. I began to say, 'Okay, you're oversensitive. You're taking rejection too much to heart. You have to disengage your ego.' It's like ducks and geese that can fly in a storm and never become wet because water just rolls off their feathers.

"Imagine yourself as a famous actor or actress in a play. In your personal life, you've just been told that a loved one has passed away. And the depression deepens throughout the day, and now it's 8 p.m. and the lights dim and the curtain rises and all of a sudden you've got to hit a switch in your head. I think that the major reason people succeed in selling is because they decide to be not the person they are, but who they need to be to succeed.

"I love playing chess. Whenever I'm losing at chess, I consistently succeed if I get up and stand behind my opponent and see the board from his side. Then I start to discover the stupid moves I've made because I can see it from his viewpoint. The salesperson's challenge is to see the world from the prospect's viewpoint."

Salespeople are often torn between their desire to grow and move up, and the fear of failing and the intense pressure and responsibilities that come with success. In order to break free from their anxieties, worries, and doubts, salespeople must find a balance in their own minds between these conflicting emotions. This balance is a personal challenge salespeople must overcome if they want to achieve greater success.

"There are so many ways to achieve this balance. People with high expectations, for example, think they ought to have no margin of error. They have to be perfect all the time. They go into selling and realize they can't be perfect all the time. When you're experiencing high failure rates and rejection ratios, one solution is to take it one step at a time. In other words, take your expectations and break them down into separate levels, so when you take a step, if you fall you don't crash, you just trip—taking shorter steps until you eventually succeed.

"The second way to do it is shown in the movie *Working Girl*. The heroine pretended to be someone successful until she gained the confidence to be herself. So we ought to emulate people who are successful until we have the qualities to help us bridge the gap.

"The third approach is knowing how to discipline ourselves so that no matter what we go through we become more resilient. Our ego is very vulnerable because it's got a sensing device. If it tends to be over-sensitive, you become too intense and this causes all of our disruptive difficulties. We need to strengthen our ego so that it sheds rejection the way ducks' feathers shed raindrops. Another analogy is that ducks and geese fly above storm clouds.

"What we need to do is keep our expectations high and learn how to raise our self-image, strengthen our ego. We can do it by faking it. We can do it by taking it one step at a time. We can do it by becoming like ducks and geese that fly above the clouds. We can do it by changing our attitude toward failure.

"We can do it by experiencing the frustration and capitalizing on it. Say, 'Hey, this is a maturing process. I've got to go through this pain in order to grow up.' Nothing can shock us in life if we're mature enough to know that what's about to happen is normal. That's why, as an example, when you're going on a trip, you check the weather forecast first. You wouldn't want to plan something and get caught in the middle of a storm, hurricane, or blizzard.

"And equally, when you go into selling, you should prepare for the storm. You should predict ahead of time where your difficulties might occur. So when they start to occur, you're not shocked, you're not in the middle of it. If you see a problem looming on the horizon, you can start to prepare yourself."

All the sales training in the world won't help if you allow rejection to overwhelm you. Becoming defensive, depressed, or discouraged by rejection will make it impossible to use your sales training successfully. By raising your level of awareness, you can have more control over your feelings, thoughts, and behavior, and that will translate into sales success.

"We need to work on two words: monitor and modify. We monitor our feelings and modify our behavior. So the monitoring begins the process. For example, I run in marathons. It's very important in marathons to monitor how you're feeling, to check yourself frequently and ask, 'Am I getting dehydrated, do I have a blister someplace, should I change my stride to reduce the pressure?' Otherwise the blister will get worse and you'll never finish.

"Well, in selling we also need to monitor our progress. We need to check on it throughout the day. We need to ask ourselves, 'How am I thinking? How am I feeling? Am I being productive or protective?' Monitor the thinking, feeling, and behavior, and then modify any of the three that need improving.

"On the other hand, positive thinking can be dangerous if it gets us psychologically into a situation that our feelings and emotions can't deal with. So for that reason we need to develop a thought process that deals very uniquely with our own situation.

"That's why when we teach a salesperson to deal with rejection, we need to give the person a series of alternative solutions so she can say, 'Well, this one fits me.' Sometimes the simplest solution is faking it. It works for a lot of people, even though it's superficial. But somebody else will be stubborn and think that you've got to suffer and become more resilient. Some people think negatively to create just enough stress to stimulate them into action."

There are two major emotions that people can use effectively in selling. One is aggression; the other is love. Hundreds of sales trainers demand that salespeople be aggressive and tell them they must have a killer instinct. Others insist you have to be caring and nurturing. In reality, sales success requires finding the right balance between the aggressiveness and sensitivity.

Art Mortell's Techniques to Achieve Your Goals

1. **Positive affirmation.** Stating positively to yourself who you are and what you can do; for example, "I enjoy jogging at least a mile per day."

2. **Description.** Describe the kind of person you want to be. The better you describe the route to your goal, the greater your chance of believing the positive affirmation and behaving accordingly.
3. **Fear.** The better we understand the negatives we will experience if we do not achieve our objectives, the more we will be motivated to strive until we succeed.
4. **Benefits.** The more we sell ourselves on what we will gain if we succeed, the more likely we are to persevere.
5. **Vivid imagination.** The subconscious mind follows what you believe to be true whether real or imagined. For example, "I see myself making the presentation, visualize myself creating a positive impact on others, and imagine myself gaining that agreement."
6. **Reward.** Decide on the gift that you will give yourself if you succeed or are in the process of achieving your objectives.
7. **Honesty.** Your defense mechanisms may be so strong that, while protecting you, they may also be blocking you from your objective. By being honest with yourself and determining what your defense mechanisms are, you will be able to accept the responsibility you have to yourself to strive forward.
8. **Forced scheduling.** Create a schedule, such as one for appointments, that forces you to perform.
9. **Commitment to others.** Here, you reverse the fear of rejection and have it work for you by obliging yourself to someone who is important to you; for example, "To ensure that I will go running early in the morning, I promised my friend that I will meet him in a certain time and place."
10. **Competition.** It often challenges us in a way that makes us operate at peak effort; for example, "I will challenge someone who is in the same position I am to a month's contest. Whoever does better wins a dinner at an agreed-upon restaurant."
11. **Leadership.** By helping someone else accomplish something of value, you can often accomplish something for yourself. For example, if you're having trouble prospecting an hour per day, find someone who is not doing it and show him how to succeed.
12. **Challenge thinking.** Instead of viewing an obstacle as a problem, think of it as an opportunity to prove how good you really are.

"In selling you have two objectives: relationships and results. Sensitivity creates the relationship; aggressiveness creates the results. There are many factors that determine how we create the balance. One factor is where you are in the selling process. If we assume that the sale begins with establishing rapport, then sensitivity is primary in developing relationships. As you move toward the close, aggressiveness becomes more important. But we must have both at the same time.

"If we're selling a product that is very simple, like magazine subscriptions, and it's being done over the phone, the aggressiveness can be stronger. There's minimal need for a relationship. If we're selling such complex products as computer technology or financial services, however, we need a far stronger relationship before we can ask for the order.

"In other words, we have to go through a greater need analysis. People must feel closer to us and trust us. We must understand their problems more thoroughly. It's all a relationship process, so we need to tip the relationship scale on the love side. I use love in a broad sense—trust, sensitivity, concern, sincerity.

"We need to create great relationships in order to get good results. Relationships are created by being a warm, sensitive, loving person. But results are gained by an aggressive, dominant personality. We need to be able to balance these two. The more balanced we are, the more effective we are. So balance is the answer, but balance must be modified according to the person you're dealing with and not according to the product you're selling and where you are in the sales process.

"Again, we must monitor and modify. Monitor the reactions of the prospect and modify your technique."

Creativity can play an important role in sales success. The ability to respond quickly to your prospect's feelings and needs can often mean the difference between a successful sales call and a failed effort.

"Creativity depends on what you're selling. If you're selling something that is very simple over the phone and making many calls, then it's almost a distraction to be creative. However, the more sophisticated the product and the market, as in selling computer technology or financial services, the greater the demand for creativity. You must be able to see the world from that prospect's viewpoint, be able to change terminology to fit his or her style, and be able to develop a unique terminology that communicates concepts clearly.

"Today in selling we've got to stop using flip charts. We've got to stop using overheads [and PowerPoint presentations]. When you're courting someone—let's say you're on a first date—you don't bring overheads, you don't bring an outline with you, you don't have notes in front of you, you don't do handouts. I think if we're going to really sell successfully, we've got to drop all the audiovisual devices. We've got to make it a conversation. We've got to bring humor into it. We've got to force ourselves into a sponta-neous love type of relationship. The greater the relationship, the better the results are going to be. The relationship is where selling begins.

"So you've got to be very creative in the sense that you disengage your own ego and totally tune into the other person's needs from his viewpoint, from his side of the table. And then be creative in chang-ing terminology so that what we're selling doesn't need to be shown because it comes alive just from the word pictures we create. Even when it comes to giving a lecture, some of the best humor comes from word pictures so your audience can visualize it happening.

"We talk about repetition being so important in selling, but it's not. For example, people from my generation remember when John Kennedy was assassinated. You can remember how you found out, where you were, how you felt and the way you reacted at that exact moment. It's so vivid in your mind years later. And it didn't require any repetition. You never needed to experience it again to remember that moment years ago.

"When I'm giving a lecture, my objective is to create such a real life experience, such an emotional impact, that they never have to hear me speak again to remember what I said. And I have people who will tell me when I'm sitting in an airplane, 'I heard you 20 years ago; you made a change in my life.' They give me word for word—very nearly—of what I said. It's changed over the years; it isn't really the way I said it, possibly. But in their minds that vividness is still there. And it's because I was successful in creating word pictures, creatively personalizing the material to their needs and making it come alive for them. It didn't require the repetition. Repetition is when you're teaching something that people aren't interested in and it must be pounded into their heads. This is fine only if you're working in a factory on an assembly line or doing canned presentations for a very simple product over the phone."

There are three primary ingredients to success in any job: a strong self-image, high expectations, and an ego resiliency to handle failure and rejection.

"Self-image is such an elusive factor. It's how we see ourselves, our sense of identity, our sense of value, our sense of importance, our viewpoint of ourselves, who we are. We don't have one self-image; we have many self-images. We can look at it in three categories. We have positive self-images about how we feel about ourselves: 'I can do this very well.' We have negative self-images: 'I'm not good at these things.' Then we have this vague area in between that we're not certain of. But I'm saying that for everything imaginable in our lives we have a self-image. If we do something we've never done before . . . we even have an image in that area, based on similar experiences.

"To strengthen your self-image, you might discuss your problem with people openly. When you discuss a problem, the less fear you feel, the more capable you feel to resolve it. We must recognize that our fears have power and yet they are invisible. We must either disengage or disarm our fears. You ask, 'How can we do that?' Often it's just by telling people about them. Sometimes just expressing the fear negates its power by exposing it to light. So there are many ways to do it. Express your fear, have role models, take each fear apart and examine its component parts. Take it a step at a time.

"Sometimes the answer may be as simple as taking an acting class. Today professional salespeople and those in management are finding that taking acting classes is one of the best ways to develop and improve their self-images, because, regardless of their feelings, they learn to play different roles. There are even consultants—experts who have a background in theater—who specialize in offering such instruction."

4 Positive Addictions That Can Help You Thrive on Anxiety

My philosophy is that to be happy, you must have four things in life. They are all crucial: health, money, love, and peace of mind. To put it another way:

1. **Exercise.** Jogging, swimming, cycling, brisk walking, rowing, canoeing, aerobic dancing, and so on. Convert anxiety into energy that gives you a sense of achievement. Realize that stress is not a killer—only the reactions to stress. Only by being in good physical condition can we enjoy everything else.
2. **Work.** Take your work home with you. Then if you get irritable, get some work done. The job is not using you, you are using the job for a sense of achievement.
3. **Relationships.** Ask your boss for advice, brainstorm with an associate, or counsel with a friend. Express your frustrations to a neighbor and have quality time with loved ones. Play out feelings with someone you are close to.
4. **Solitary Activities.** Read a book, watch a sunset, play a musical instrument, meditate or become spiritual.

You can be addicted to a positive attitude as easily as a negative one. You must have all four each day. Realize the connection between the four positive addictions. You need all four in order to stay in balance. And if we're not in balance, then we become, to varying degrees, self-destructive. For example, if people place great emphasis on money, they may lose love relationships, they may lose their health or their peace of mind. Be aware of the importance of balance.

To succeed in selling requires being a laser beam that has three parts to it: intensity, concentration, and focus. We need to know how to flip switches in our heads each day, to switch from one laser beam to the other. I'm saying you need four laser beams each day to be happy.

And so, number one, I go out running, for my health. Then I give my lectures, as I'll be doing this afternoon and that's my livelihood. And then there's time to call home and talk to my family or to work on my new book. If they are traveling with me, we'll have dinner and go out to a movie. Late in the evening is time to take a walk in the moonlight and read a book before I fall asleep, write poetry, and be meditative and focus on my inner needs and solitude.

It's fascinating to realize that within the mind there are many compartments. And we need to learn how to walk the corridors of our minds and be able to pick and choose which room we prefer at any given time.

Creativity helps to strengthen relationships; a strong self-image helps to handle rejection. Both are essential ingredients for sales success.

"A lot of our interpersonal creativity is really not creativity at all but a series of computerized modules in our mind from past successes in which we, as a director of the show, are hitting buttons at high speed and giving the actor on the stage the lines to use. We have this little voice in the back of our minds saying, 'This great line last year would work super right now.' We have high-speed spontaneity. We can't have that kind of spontaneity if we have a negative self-image or if we have fears of rejection. So to be able to have this kind of fluidity requires a strong self-image and then an amusement with rejection.

"In other words, we know that if we take a chance and wipe out, it's going to be kind of funny rather than a disastrous experience. If we think, 'Disastrous experience, whoa, I better not take a chance,' we may lose spontaneity. But the spontaneity might not be so creative. In reality, our ability to make high-speed changes in our computerized modules—to pick number 7A or number 12B—may be the important quality.

"Children are very creative without having the modules in their head to choose from because they haven't had the experiences yet. And children have a spontaneity because they know ahead of time they're going to be loved automatically for whatever they say. They're also great role players. In other words, they're on stage all the time.

They're playing improvisation. So what we need to do is develop the improvisation skills and the spontaneity of a creative child.

"What that really means is having no fear of rejection while still being sensitive to the person you're dealing with."

In his lectures, Mortell seeks to change people's perceptions of reality. He tries to help them see that failure does not exist and wants them instead to realize that the reality they experience is always for their benefit. The goal is to develop entirely new reactions to rejection—to capitalize on it.

"Very simply, we have two major solutions. One is psychological. Like ducks and geese that can fly in a storm and never get wet from the rain, we can be traveling toward our objective in the middle of a storm and never become depressed by the rejection.

"We can fly above the clouds, which means raising our self-image and deciding everything is petty, everything is like an amusement to us. Or we can have the raindrops just roll off our feathers so we disengage the ego. And even though we're in the middle of the storm, not flying above it but in the middle of it, we can protect our self-image by disengaging our ego and still stay in motion as we move toward our goals.

"The second solution is behavioral. People can think negatively. They can be depressed. They can still succeed. They can behave as they need to regardless of how they think or feel."

Success in sales is fundamentally a matter of overcoming resistance. In many ways, the entire objective in sales is to deal with resistance.

"We can look at resistance as a varying degree of tension. All the reasons why people don't buy become points of resistance, and as tension increases they become like invisible walls—all these walls of tension. And so maybe the primary objective in selling is to eliminate resistance and increase receptivity, and that requires knowing how to disengage from the tension. So how do we get rid of tension? We can get rid of tension by establishing rapport. What does that mean? Being friendly, being sensitive, caring, seeing the world from the other person's viewpoint and creating word pictures, being spontaneous and creative.

"We can also relieve tension through humor. Some people, including myself, are not humorous by nature. If we can disengage our fear of rejection and allow ourselves to be spontaneous, then the humor comes to us naturally.

"As an example, we know that many aggressive, dominant people have difficulty staying hostile or aggressive over lunch or dinner. So environment is a factor. People have different personalities at work than they have at home. So get them in more of a home environment over lunch or dinner.

"The second approach would be to bring humor into it. Many people will not laugh at themselves but will laugh heartily at somebody else. That's why Rodney Dangerfield is so good. He laughs at himself, and we can enjoy that because he's not attacking us.

"Personally, I like simple lines. I like to reduce the pressure by saying humorously: 'How about if I call you five years from now?' I'm actually telling people why I'm enjoying their hostility, why it's a benefit to me. 'I've been doing so well lately that I really appreciate your working me over like this. I haven't had a challenge like this in a couple of months. I've been losing my sharpness. I really could use this. Thanks a lot. Can I call you every time I'm feeling good, and you can work me over?' If we phrase it properly, that technique will work with any hostile prospect.

"Sometimes the simplest things work so well. For example, I often tell this story: Imagine a barracuda and a mackerel in the same pool of water together. A barracuda just loves mackerel. The only thing he does not know is that in between him and the mackerel is a great big piece of glass. The barracuda takes off like a shot and—wham—hits the glass. He has no idea what he hit, so he reels around and tries again. Wham—into the glass! After a while he looks at the mackerel and gets a headache just looking at it. And that 'gets a headache' creates an audience response.

"As a personal example, I'll never forget when I was real young, out in the ocean for a day, and it was really quiet in the water. I had a ball with me, and I lost it. The current began taking it away. I began to walk out, trying to catch up to the ball, but when the water reached my waist, I got frightened and went back.

"Later in the day, I was getting more and more used to the water and was walking further out, up to my ears and nose. And Mom said to me, 'Now Arthur, if you were as confident this morning as you are now, you would have gotten the ball back easily.' The idea is that we often condition ourselves to back off at certain points. As time goes by we may gain confidence, but we still avoid the same challenge because the conditioning, even with the new confidence, keeps us from a breakthrough. Simple thoughts, simple ideas."

Resistance . . . where would salespeople be without it? It's been said that without resistance, the world would cease to spin, rain would stop falling to earth, the seasons would disappear, sticks rubbed together would never make a fire, teeth could not grind food, tires would not grip the road. Without resistance, selling just wouldn't be. So look for that argumentative prospect, that irate customer, that reluctant client, that hesitant buyer, that procrastinating purchasing agent. They're your opportunities to sell!

ACTION STEPS

CONFIDENCE

1. There are four methods for achieving balance: taking things one step at a time, faking it, building resilience, and preparation. Find one that works for you.
2. To effectively handle rejection, constantly monitor your own mental state with probing self-questions.
3. Selling requires that you open with love and close assertively. Build rapport and trust at the beginning of the sale with love, then close the deal with asserting what you believe.
4. Find creative mental images that stir your customers' emotions. Don't be repetitive. Be effective.
5. Allow yourself to be spontaneous. This will bring out your humorous side and help you build rapport and trust among your prospects.

Chapter 5

Creativity: Nine Ways to Be Innovative in Selling

Objective:
To help you get in touch with your personal creativity to improve your product, service, or selling strategy and find better customer solutions.

Synopsis:
1. Being "practical" and "following the rules" are counterproductive to innovative thinking.
2. The power of people's ideas is a manager's most important resource.
3. Creative thinking builds self-esteem and fires enzymes in the brain that produce a natural high.
4. Without proper guidance, it is extremely difficult to develop creative thinking patterns that produce new ideas.
5. Everything new is some manipulation of something that already exists.

Masaru Ibuka, honorary chairman of Sony, took a failed tape recorder and:

- Eliminated the recorder function altogether.
- Added lightweight portable headphones to magnify the sound.
- Modified the marketing introduction. Sony gave away free samples to celebrities and put their press announcement on cassette.
- Found another market for it by marketing it as a new entertainment concept.

The result? The Walkman tape player, one of the biggest product successes in modern times, the result of a "failed" product, was born.

Ibuka had taken a failed product and, by manipulating it, asking questions about it, refusing to see its limitations, invented a product that introduced the world to "headphone culture."

In hindsight, the idea of a Walkman seems obvious. Its very obviousness makes it so infuriating. All great ideas seem obvious in hindsight. But how in the world do people discover them?

How did Fred Smith get the hub-and-spoke transportation idea that led to Federal Express?

What led Thomas Monaghan of Domino's Pizza to market and guarantee speed of delivery?

What inspired 3M's Arthur Fry to think of a use for an adhesive that made the Post-it pads possible?

How did Steve Jobs get his ideas to raise the capital and start Apple Computer to compete against IBM?

How can you be the one who comes up with the next great idea in sales or marketing?

Have you ever tried to get a new idea simply by choosing to have one?

Spend a few minutes and see how many new ways you can think of to sell your product. How did you do? If you're like most of us, you probably had difficulty coming up with more than a few. Our minds generally don't cooperate in such matters. It is very hard for us simply to will new ideas without some kind of intermediate step. However, when you use a checklist of idea-spurring questions, it's a snap to generate new ideas, solutions, breakthroughs, or whatever you need.

This chapter, based on the work of Alex Osborn, a pioneer teacher of creativity and father of brainstorming, and Michael

---

Expert Advice: This chapter features contributions from Michael Michalko. He is one the most highly acclaimed creativity experts in the world and author of the best seller *Thinkertoys, ThinkPak,* and *Cracking Creativity* (www .creativethinking.net).

Michalko's book *Thinkertoys: A Handbook of Business Creativity for the '90s,* contains a checklist of idea-spurring questions to help anyone uncover the creativity that rests just beneath the brain's surface. Everything new is some manipulation of something that already exists. To create something new (idea, product, service, process, or whatever you need), all you have to do is take a subject and manipulate it in some fashion. There are nine principal ways to manipulate a subject. To help folks remember them, the nine ways are arranged here into the following mnemonic:

S	Substitute?
C	Combine?
A	Adapt?
M	Magnify? Modify?
P	Put to other uses?
E	Eliminate or Minimize?
R	Rearrange or Reverse?

These questions give conscious direction to your creativity. Instead of trying to juggle several concepts in your mind, hoping that an idea will somehow magically appear, ask questions to focus your imagination on the subject. When you focus on a question, you have to think about it. And when you ask yourself the right question, you have to think up, as well as think about, something.

Ibuka took the "failed" recorder and asked, "What can be eliminated?" "What can be added?" "How can I magnify the sound?" and "How can I modify the marketing introduction so that I stay within a small budget?" and created the Walkman.

You, too, can find creative new ideas to sell your product with SCAMPER questions. As you read the rest of this article, answer the questions as they occur, and ask yourself how you can improve the way you sell.

SUBSTITUTE?

The principle of substitution is a sound way to develop alternative ideas to anything that exists. Think up ways of changing this for that and that for this. You can substitute things, places, procedures, people, ideas, and even emotions. It is a trial-and-error method of replacing one thing with another until you find the right idea. Ask:

- What can be substituted in your selling process? Can you substitute someone else? Can you substitute something else?
- Can you change the place?
- What would happen if you used another approach?
- What if you used a different procedure?
- Can you change the rules about selling in your organization?
- Can you use other materials to help you sell?
- Can you change your viewpoint about the way you sell?

Example: Can you substitute someone else? Garden Way, the manufacturer of high-end Troy-Bilt rototillers, used to substitute customers for part of its print advertising program. The company recruited them, at the time of their purchase, into its Good Neighbor program by offering them a special deal on their purchase. Garden Way then listed them in a directory. Garden Way then put prospective buyers in touch with a volunteer neighbor who owned a rototiller so the buyer could test drive the machine and query the customer.

COMBINE?

Much creative thinking involves combining previously unrelated subjects and creating something new. The printing press was created by Gutenberg, who combined the coin punch with the wine press. Mathematics was combined with biology by Gregor Mendel to create the discipline of genetics. The process of combining ideas or elements or parts of ideas is called synthesis. Synthesis is regarded by many to be the essence of creativity. Ask:

- What different ideas about selling can be combined?
- Can you combine purposes with someone or something else?
- Combine units?
- How about a combination in packaging?
- What can be combined to multiply possible uses?
- Can you combine appeals with something else?
- Can you provide an assortment, an ensemble, a variety?

Example: What can be combined to multiply the purposes? A salesman bought a failing retail store that sold video cameras. The salesman contracted with the local amusement park to operate a small booth next to the main ticket booth. There, for a special price, you buy a ticket to the park and rent a video camera. He demonstrates how to shoot video. The customer spends the day filming his children. Later, the salesman provides refreshments, shows the video, praises the customer's talents, counsels the customer on how to improve, and asks for the customer's phone number. A few weeks later, he calls the prospect and announces a special discount sale. If the prospect still fails to buy, he waits two months and then comes to his house, bringing a toy for the prospect's child and shoots another demo around the house. Finally, he shows the video on the prospect's own television. By combining a retail operation with an amusement rental service, he has turned a failed operation into a successful one. Sales are booming.

ADAPT?

One of the paradoxes of creativity is that in order to think originally, we must first familiarize ourselves with the ideas of others. Thomas Edison put it this way: "Make it a habit to keep on

TIPS

7 ADDITIONAL TIPS ON CREATIVITY

1 Be dissatisfied with the status quo. Dissatisfaction fuels creativity.

2 Be silly. Understand that to come up with creative solutions, you may have to go out on a limb and expose yourself to appearing ridiculous.

3 Wait for the right solution. Rather than going with the first possible answer, come up with more. Then, with all these possible solutions, pick the best among them.

4 Innovative solutions need not be radical departures from convention. Often, a minor change or addition to a product can increase its value and utility exponentially.

5 To be creative, try to approach a problem or dilemma from a completely different perspective. Think of someone who is completely different from you. How would he or she approach this problem?

6 Look at the problem and imagine adding or subtracting a part. How does this change the whole? What else could be added, subtracted, or substituted? Follow these changes to their likely conclusion. How does this affect the solution?

7 Try working backward from the desired result to a workable model of your product or service. Often, this perspective opens up a whole avenue of possibilities.

the lookout for novel and interesting ideas that others have used successfully. Your idea needs to be original only in its adaptation to the problem you are working on." Ask:

- What else is like your product? How is it sold? Does it suggest any new ideas?
- Does the past offer a parallel you could use? What has worked before?
- What could you copy? Is there something similar you could partially copy?
- Whom could you emulate? What have others done? What have experts done?
- What different or unusual contexts can you put your product in? Historical context? Future context?
- What ideas can you adapt from the world of sports? Television? Books? Politics? Movies? Religion?

Example: What could you copy? A Princeton, New Jersey, saleswoman who sells magazine subscriptions figured out how to make subscriptions an impulse item by adapting an idea from the way stereo accessories are sold. Stereo accessories are sold in colorful packages that hang from retail racks or spinning racks. She boxes her gift subscription forms with greeting cards and displays them on spinning racks in shops. Retailers get a new impulse item; publishers get a cheap way to add new readers. Sales have exploded.

MAGNIFY?

An easy way to create a new idea is to take a subject and add something to it. Computer manufacturers are constantly adding more features, promoting greater speed, and extending warranties. Gas stations now sell groceries and fast food. Initially, Tom Monaghan of Domino's Pizza obliterated his competition by providing a faster, guaranteed delivery service. Ask:

- What can be added? More time? Greater frequency? Extra features?
- What strength can you add? Can you maximize existing strengths?
- What can be magnified, made larger, or extended?
- What would happen if you exaggerated? Overstated?
- What can add extra value? Can you make your product do more things?
- What can be duplicated? Doubled? Repeated?
- What's missing that could be useful? What are the gaps that have to be completed? What else do you need to know?
- How could you carry it to the dramatic extreme?

Example: Can you add more frequency? IKEA, the Swedish furniture chain, figured out a way to expand its retail traffic by renting Christmas trees. "The spirit of Christmas can't be bought, but for $10 you can rent it," the IKEA ad said. For $20—$10 for the rental and $10 for the deposit—IKEA would rent you a Douglas fir in New York City, where trees can go from $50 and up. After the holidays, customers return the tree and IKEA would mulch the tree for their garden or donate it to their community. The customer also received a coupon for a free 4-year-old blue spruce sapling to help save the environment. Customers could pick up their tree in the first week of April. That's selling! Just by being extra nice to its customers, IKEA made it worth their while to visit a store three separate times.

MODIFY?

At one time, the Ford Motor Company had 60 percent of the automobile market. General Motors asked questions about modification and came out with a philosophy that stated, "A car with every shape and color for every purse and purpose." Henry Ford responded with, "Any customer can have a car painted any color so long as it is black." Ford's sales slumped, and by the 1940s the company had just 20 percent of the new car market. GM, by modifying their products to the market, soon took the lead. What can be modified? Just about any aspect of anything. Ask:

- How can you alter the way you sell for the better?
- What can be modified about the way you sell?
- Can you change meaning, name, color, form, shape?
- Can you give it a new twist?
- What doesn't feel right? What can you do differently?
- What changes can be made in the sales plans? In the process?
- In what other form could you present your product?
- Can the package be combined with the form?
- Can you change your perspective? How would your teacher look at it? Your father? Competition? Ted Koppel? Napoleon?

Example: Can you give it a new twist? Is it possible to outsmart the competitor without outspending them? Sheri Poe, founder of Ryka, Inc., found her market for women's sneakers by creating a new twist in her marketing plans. Instead of selling just her sneakers, she also sells her concept: "The first sneaker made for women, by women." Instead of concentrating her advertising efforts directly on the consumer, she markets to aerobics instructors and salespeople. In only five years the company has grown to $8 million in sales.

PUT TO OTHER USES?

Find an idea, product, or service and then imagine what else you can do with it. A subject takes its meaning from the context in which you put it. Change the context and you change the meaning. George

Washington Carver, botanist and chemist, discovered more than 300 uses for the lowly peanut by constantly looking for new uses. Ask:

- In what other ways could your product be used?
- Are there new ways to use it as is?
- Can you make it do more things? Can you find other benefits?
- Can you modify it in some fashion to fit a new use?
- What's being wasted that can be put to use?
- Other extensions? Spinoffs?
- Other markets?

Example: Are there new ways to use it as is? In 1956, the Jacuzzi brothers, who sold water pumps for farm use, designed a special whirlpool bath as a treatment for their cousin's arthritis. They sold a few for other victims. It wasn't until 1968 that Roy Jacuzzi discovered another use and another market for it—the luxury bath market—and bathrooms were never the same again. The Jacuzzi sold like crazy across the country from California to the White House.

ELIMINATE?

New ideas are sometimes found when you subtract something from your subject. Through repeated trimming of ideas, objects, and processes, one gradually narrows it down to that part or function that is really necessary or makes it appropriate for another use. For instance, if you omit the warlike function from a tank and keep only the caterpillar track, you create a tractor. Ask:

- What should you omit from the way you sell?
- Should you divide anything? Split up?
- What's not necessary? What isn't the problem? What can you leave out? Omit? Subtract? Delete?

- How can this be done better and more cheaply? Streamline?
- What if you understate?
- Can you separate your sales procedures into different parts? Can you determine the correctness of each part? Can you improve one part at a time?
- Can you eliminate the rules? Simplify? Where could you ease off?
- What if nothing is done?

Example: What should you omit from the way you sell? If you don't give massive rebates and run hundreds of millions of dollars of advertising hype, there is no way you can sell a car in America today. Right? Not so, proved Gordon Stewart, owner of Garden City Chevrolet in Garden City, Michigan. He knows that Americans do not like to bargain for a car. They always feel as if they have been had. So he did something about it. He eliminated the dickering and sold the idea of no-dickering pricing. He put red-tag final offers on the windshields of his cars. He gave the people a reason to come in and look. Some years ago, a car sticker-priced at $12,234 had a non-negotiable red-tag price of $10,408. His salespeople are paid on volume, not profit. They must sell the dealership and the car. Can you imagine a car salesperson selling a car and not price? Selling price is never selling. One year, he sold 2,079 cars to retail customers, well above the 1,125 target set by the factory.

REARRANGE?

Creativity, it could be said, consists largely of rearranging what we know in order to find out what we do not know. Rearrangement usually offers countless alternatives for ideas, goods and services. A baseball manager, for example, can shuffle his lineup 362,880 times. Ask:

- How else can you arrange things? What other arrangement might be better?
- What would happen if you interchanged components?

- Change the pattern? What other layout might be better?
- Can you change the order? Where should this be in relation to that? Change the sequence?
- Transpose cause and effect?
- How about timing? How about a change of pace? Different tempo? Change schedule? Chronologized? Systemized?
- What if you change the way you work? Change your environment? Method? People? Priorities? Habits?

Example: What happens when salespeople change the pace of their presentation? Fast-talking salespeople are sometimes regarded with suspicion, but rapid speech may actually increase one's persuasiveness. Norman Miller and his coworkers approached Los Angeles residents in parks and shopping malls and asked them to listen to a tape-recorded speech arguing that caffeine should be regarded as a dangerous drug. All subjects heard the same message, but half heard it at the slow rate of 102 words per minute and half at the fast rate of 195 words per minute. The fast-talking communicator was viewed as being the more knowledgeable and objective, and was more effective at changing the subject's attitudes. Within limits, the faster you talk, the more likely people are to assume you know what you're talking about.

REVERSE?

Reversing your perspective on your ideas, goods, or services opens your thinking. Look at opposites and you'll see things you normally miss. Ask "What is the opposite of this?" to find a new way of looking at things. The historical breakthroughs of Columbus and Copernicus were the polar opposites of the current beliefs of their day. Many creative people get their most original ideas when they reverse a subject. Ask:

- How can you reverse the way you look at selling? Turn it around? What happens when you play devil's advocate?

- Can you turn the negatives into positives? Reframe them?
- What are the opposites? What happens when they are reversed? Reverse assumptions? Roles? Relationships? Uses? Functions? Ideas?
- Can you consider it backward? Work from the desired result backward to the subject?
- What if you do the unexpected? What surprises can you pull? How can you turn the tables?

Example: Reverse assumptions. The Williams Companies had 28,000 miles of oil pipeline all over the country. When they were looking to move into new businesses, they assumed they had to find something they could pump through the pipes. Nothing worked. Finally, a salesman said, "How about not pumping anything through the pipes?" He then asked various companies if they had any use for 28,000 miles of empty oil pipelines. One day he called MCI and discovered they could run their fiber-optic cables through the pipes. Williams sold the idea to MCI, and the rest is history.

Instability has become almost a way of life in today's world because of frantic social, business, and technological changes. This instability means that fresh ideas will become the most precious raw materials in the world. Salespeople need to think on their own, to produce new ideas, and to take responsibility for their own destiny. This question checklist may be the tool that will open your mind to create the idea that will revolutionize the way you sell and your life.

ACTION STEPS

CREATIVITY

1. Don't let complacency ruin your powers for creative thinking.
2. Discover what times of day are your most creative and use this time to find innovative solutions.
3. Find as many answers to a problem as possible. The more possible solutions, the more likely the right solution will be discovered.
4. Incorporate solutions from other fields than your own. Often, innovative ideas stem from unexpected sources.

Chapter 6

Energy: Getting Fired Up to Sell

Objective:

To explain the unique properties of energy to enable you to focus your finite amount of energy to accomplish your dreams.

Synopsis:

1. Whether in motion or standing still, we expend energy.
2. To get where we want to go, it is better to expend energy wisely than to waste it on fruitless ventures.
3. Energy problems occur when you are unsure of your goal, fail to see obstacles in your way, or chase your goal unprepared.

Y ou need as much energy to achieve nothing in life as you need to achieve something, according to A. R. Stielau-Pallas, who offers suggestions for making you more energy efficient. The road to success has many destinations. The choices seem limitless, but what you need is a decision. A halfhearted effort toward an unclear goal will use energy. It will not achieve results. What you need is direction and commitment.

Imagine yourself taking a vacation. You arrive at the town's main intersection. The signs indicate many possible destinations. But you haven't decided where to go. So you sit with your motor running, and eventually run out of gas. You have used time and energy but have accomplished nothing. Or suppose you have several places you'd like to visit. You head toward the first place. Then you change your mind, make a u-turn, and start off toward your new destination. Now you run into rush hour traffic and redirect your trip again. Your gas tank is almost empty, so you take the next exit and pull into a service station. You realize that you are back where you began! With the same amount of energy you could have reached any one of your choices.

Maybe you decide to take a trip to attend a niece's wedding, despite an important deadline at work. You don't figure out how much gas you will need, or how many hours it will take to get there—you just get going. After driving until you're exhausted, you pull over to refuel and get a map. At this point, you realize (1) you really can't afford this trip and (2) even if you reach your goal, you won't have time to get back and meet your deadline.

In all of these cases you have expended energy without reaching your destination. Deciding on your goal, concentrating on only that goal, recognizing obstacles, and recognizing extra energy needs to attain your goal are all fundamental to achievement. This holds true whether it is an actual destination, a business quota, or a personal dream you are trying to reach.

Maybe you're great at planning and taking trips. So let's use another example. You are attending a convention. It is dinner time and the hotel has provided a large buffet. You will notice several indecisive "types" as they move through the line.

There are those who don't know what they want yet, passing many dishes, waiting to see if something better is ahead of them. When they reach the end, they discover that they haven't gotten anything and must start over again.

Some can't decide what they want, so they take a little of everything. When they reach the end of the line and discover their favorite foods, their plates are already overfull.

Expert Advice: This chapter features contributions from Alfred R. Stielau-Pallas.

Then there are those who would rather let someone else go through the line for them. They say they don't really care what they get. However, when they do get their plates, they'll complain about what they did and didn't get.

Still another type will be so busy watching what and how much of everything everyone else is getting that they don't know they've missed their favorites until they've passed them.

Again, everyone used the same amount of energy to move through the line. But only those who decided what they wanted, concentrated on those dishes, recognized that they only had room on their plates for some things, and recognized that going slowly the first time might save them an extra trip achieved their goal—a pleasant meal.

I suggest a step-by-step approach to determine which of your goals is really the most important to you. Take one piece of paper for each goal, dividing it into pro and con columns. As you list all of the advantages and disadvantages of achieving this goal, give each idea a rating from 1 to 10. If you want a promotion, which will mean a pay increase (7) and more prestige (8), but will mean more travel (8) and less time with your family (10), you end up with a score of 15:18. With a score this close, leaning toward the negative, you may only *think* that this promotion is what you want. However, a concrete image of what you can expect, both pro and con, after accomplishing this particular goal, will make your decision easier and more realistic.

Once you have decided on your number one goal, it is important to follow through. Following are some brief examples that show how failures happen when your energy is not concentrated on a single aim:

- A tennis player is interested in his appearance more than his performance; his attention is on the crowd, not on the game.
- An auto worker makes more mistakes, or is careless, on Mondays and Fridays; he is thinking about or recovering from the weekend.
- A person with a heart condition is put on a diet but gains weight again; he is still meeting appetite goals, not health goals.

Let's say you have decided on your major goal and are really concentrating on it. But you're still having problems. You may have too many obstacles in the way. An adventurous jungle safari may be a lifelong dream, but won't be fun if it produces more anxiety than pleasure. Fear of vaccination, snake bites, or attacks by wild animals may have to be overcome before making this trip a realistic goal.

Next, you must recognize that the extra energy needed to meet your goal must come from other areas. You will need to sacrifice time and put aside other aims. This is much easier if your goal is your own and not someone else's. If you paint the house because it's good exercise or will look nice, you'll finish quickly. It won't matter that you didn't mow the lawn and wash the windows. But if your spouse, the neighbors, or your mother-in-law made the decision, you'll lack the internal drive to keep going. You'll do other chores you'd rather do, or take lots of breaks. The house many never get completely painted!

To benefit from "The Right Use of Energy," you need to recognize some basic energy rules and use them to your own advantage:

- Energy goes into what seems most important, so decide what is most important.
- Energy is limited, so concentrate on one goal.
- Energy for one goal is taken from others, so recognize the pros and cons, and be realistic.
- Energy is used regardless of direction, so change "I don't care" and "I don't know" to "I know" and "I care."
- Energy is nontransferable, so recognize the difference between your goals and others' goals for you.
- On the road to success, you can idle, go in circles, or reach your destination using the same amount of energy. Deciding what you want, then pursuing it is the first step toward a long journey of achievement.

ACTION STEPS

ENERGY

1. To discover which of your goals deserves your attention, list all the pros and cons of achieving each goal. Then give each idea a rating from 1 to 10. This will help you determine which goals are most important.
2. Eliminate the internal obstacles between you and your goal. If you are subconsciously impeding your own progress, you will be spinning your wheels.
3. Remember that energy for one goal is taken from others. Decide early on which goal is worthy of your full energy investment.
4. Determine exactly how much energy you will need to expend to achieve your goal. Sacrifice some other goals to achieve the primary one. No great goal has ever been achieved without sacrifice.

Chapter 7

Goals: Establish a Clear Track to Your Destination

Objective:

To learn how to set realistic goals—and the process to achieve them—to help you fulfill your long-term dreams.

Synopsis:

1. A sales rep with all the right tools will still flounder without the direction that definitive goals provide.
2. Goals translate directly into positive action.
3. Long-term goals help you move beyond inevitable short-term frustrations.
4. Long-term goals should be broken down into smaller, sustaining goals.
5. Your goals should make you proud when you accomplish them.

Tryon Edwards once said: "Thoughts lead on to purposes; purposes go forth into action; actions form habits; habits decide character; and character fixes destiny." Recently, while conducting a sales seminar, I asked, "How many of you have written out your goals?" The results were stunning. Of 123 salespeople present, only three admitted to writing down their goals. I find that alarming.

Proper goal setting and good execution of those goals automatically solves many important problems for salespeople. Once goals have been set, the salesperson can translate them into positive action. Then the salesperson automatically becomes well organized by doing things in the order of their importance. Finally, that salesperson develops good working habits and becomes self-disciplined.

Goal-minded salespeople never take their minds off of long-range goals, because the penalty—short-term frustrations—can wipe out a haphazard plan. It is simple to set goals and establish a positive track to run on. Yet, in my opinion, 95 percent of salespeople work without any plan to follow. They are merely going this way one day and that way the next day, with no exact target in mind. This is nothing less than sheer folly, since it's as impossible to hit something you have never seen (a target) as it is to return from somewhere you have never been.

William Jennings Bryan commented about goals and destiny by saying: "Destiny is not a matter of chance, it is a matter of choice; it is not a thing to be waited for, it is a thing to be achieved."

Salespeople who have no specific goals that they are interested in and committed to achieving go around in circles feeling lost and professionally purposeless. People who say that life is not worthwhile are really saying that they have no worthwhile goals. Goals should be realistic, personal, and worthy. They should justify the effort it takes to achieve them. They should stand for something worth working for. They should make you proud when you have accomplished them.

To accurately and honestly determine your present situation, know exactly where you now stand, where you want to go, and what you can realistically expect in the future. This does not take into account what you might win in a lottery, where you thought you would be by this time last year, or what you vaguely think you're really worth if only prospects would pay attention to you. Look at yourself honestly and squarely. What do I want to do and what do I want to be? Do I want a promotion? Do I want a business of my own? What are my resources? Do I want to change fields?

Expert Advice: This chapter features contributions from Grant Gard, the accomplished author of several books, including *The Art of Confident Public Speaking* and *Championship Selling*.

What do I have to do to get there? What are my strengths, and where are my weaknesses? How much money do I want to make? What do I want to provide my family—home, education, car, vacation, insurance? Make a complete list of the facts and then study it.

To set and define your realistic, worthy goals, use crystallized thinking. Looking at your list, decide your overall major goal. Aim high, have great expectations, but know that every journey begins with a single step and most journeys only end by putting one foot in front of the other.

The very minute you write out your goals, dedicate yourself to their successful attainment. Imagine yourself succeeding, thus crowding out negative, fearful thoughts. If such thoughts do cross your consciousness, do not try to squelch them, but examine where they come from, deal with them, and then discard them as useless in your overall plan. Don't take negative thoughts personally. Dress and act the part of the successful salesperson you really want to be. Always work and live by faith and be persistent. Persistence by its very nature develops purpose, direction, and courage.

To develop a complete plan of specific activities, determine how you are going to accomplish your major and sustaining goals. Develop a plan of specific activities—what has to be done and how you are going to do it. The more specific you make this stage, the more likely you are to meet your goals. If every point is clearly defined on an hourly, daily, and weekly basis, you geometrically increase your success ratio. Major goals are accomplished by completing the sustaining goals one at a time. Your selling day will be one of organized activity. Visualize in your mind the successful completion of every sustaining goal.

Go at every activity without giving thought to the possibility of defeat. Concentrate on your strengths and not on your weaknesses. Be determined to follow through on every point in your goal achievement plan. This develops even more self-confidence in your abilities and helps you to conquer obstacles and circumstances that might get in your way. Because a heartfelt, burning desire is the most powerful motivator there is, develop your own burning desire.

Timetables and deadlines are very important to achieving goals. When do you want to achieve your goals? Don't use terms like "a long time," "shortly," "about two years," "sometime in the future," or "possibly six months." Write down the actual dates you want these goals to be a reality. Every date should be specific—nothing general, nothing fuzzy. This stops procrastination and provides you with checkpoints along your path.

Think about what you are really doing when you write out your goals. You are turning intentions into commitments, commitments into involvements, involvements into positive actions. Goals prevent drifting. Remember: Where there is no purpose, no progress follows.

To set and achieve your goals, I suggest developing a complete goal blueprint. Since everyone's circumstances are different, use the form here as a guide. Take time right now to build yourself a complete goal outline by outlining your major goal, 10 to 15 sustaining goals, and 5 to 15 specific activities you must accomplish to reach each sustaining goal.

MAJOR GOAL

I will have done an outstanding job for the next calendar year by increasing my sales commission or achieving a promotion to (title), so that my total income will be X. Then, each year thereafter, I will increase my income to X over the previous year. This will enable me to purchase (item) by (date), (item) by (date), (item) by (date).

Sustaining Goal #1   To maintain an adequate number of bona fide prospects to keep me busy selling productively all day, every day. Specific activities to do daily, weekly, monthly include:

1. Devote a minimum of four hours per week to productive prospecting.
2. Develop and maintain close contact with productive centers of influence.
3. Get leads from every person I sell.

4. Get favorable PR by speaking to one service club, church group, or company meeting per month.
5. Prospect at least two hours per week using the telephone.
6. Use the telephone or person-to-person contact to call on five present customers and ask each for names of prospects.

Sustaining Goal #2   Make X number of face-to-face presentations monthly. Specific activities to do daily, weekly, monthly include:

1. Fill each day with X number of productive appointments.
2. Fill each week with X number of productive appointments.
3. Be in the field making calls during X number of hours daily, weekly.
4. Do necessary paper work during nonproductive calling hours.
5. Have available more than an adequate number of bona fide prospects each day.
6. Preselect each day alternate cold calls to fill in any open time.
7. Make X number of face-to-face presentations daily, weekly.

Sustaining Goal #3   Increase the ratio of sales closings. Specific activities to do daily, weekly, monthly include:

1. Analyze each attempt to sell.
2. Read a book on selling X number of minutes per day.
3. Listen to audio books in between calls.
4. Review and study company sales training methods X number of times weekly.
5. Set up a definite self-improvement program.

Sustaining Goal #4   Make most productive use of time. Specific activities to do daily, weekly, monthly include:

1. Every evening plan for best utilization of time for next day.
2. Utilize phone to firm up all appointments each day.
3. Visit less and spend more time selling on each interview.

4. Permit no nonproductive use of time during prime selling hours.
5. Daily, weekly, and monthly, do things in the order of their importance.
6. Arrange appointments from a geographical standpoint.

Sustaining Goal #5 Maintain a positive, enthusiastic attitude. Specific activities to do daily, weekly, monthly include:

1. Use X number of pep talks daily.
2. Read one good book on self-improvement every month.
3. Listen daily to inspirational tapes.
4. Keep my mind on the importance of achieving my goals.
5. Be an example of an enthusiastic person.
6. Review my goals daily.

To complete a form like this for yourself requires concentrated thought and the effort of putting it down on paper or entering it into your computer. In the same way that sales calls yield better results when you are prepared, when you know the buyer and the company, the competition, and the value of your product, your goal-setting program will prove its worth if you'll give it the chance. Anything that produces real results is worth the effort you put into it.

ACTION STEPS

GOALS

1. When you write down your goals, develop a plan for specific activities to accomplish them.
2. Give yourself detailed deadlines to accomplish each goal; don't use such hazy terms as "shortly," "in about two years," or others.
3. Make goal "blueprints" listing your major goal, 10–15 sustaining goals, and 5–15 specific activities you must accomplish to reach each sustaining goal.

Chapter 8

Self-Improvement:
The Key to
Professional Growth

Objective:

To help you create a steady program for self-improvement to lead to greater success in both your professional and your personal life.

Synopsis:

1. In a competitive world, continuous success requires constant self-improvement and development.

2. The responsibility for growth always lies with the individual.

3. Beneficial changes occur not when we try to create perfection, but rather when we steadily improve on a day-to-day basis.

As a sales representative and a professional, you need to carry out a systematic and continuous plan of self-improvement. In the modern world of business and selling, competition is getting tougher and tougher. Competition for jobs is getting tougher, competition for the customer's dollar is getting tougher, the sales ability of your own competitors is getting tougher.

The only way you can survive is to get better and better, and do it faster than your competitors. Your training doesn't end at the completion of a formal training program; it only begins. A formal program will serve as no more than a launching pad for your training. As long as you are in a career of selling, you must be in a career of training, of learning, of self-development, of getting better. Of course, experience adds greatly to the development of any man or woman, but it also takes a lot of hard study and analysis to be the best you can be.

In addition to the usual sales objectives, establish monthly, quarterly, semiannual, and annual objectives for personal development. These objectives are, of course, above and beyond those activities required by your company. These are the things you plan to do on your own to make yourself more valuable to your company, to your profession, to your family, and to yourself. It is the hallmark of true professionals to constantly seek ways of becoming more professional in their work. It is a means of wringing a full year's learning from each year on the job. There is a vast difference between the salesperson who has 10 years of experience and the one who has "one year's experience 10 times." The one who is capable of making each year a learning experience is in a position to move up the corporate ladder and become a manager of others.

Personal development objectives are often established in very vague, ambiguous terms—for instance, "during the next six months I will exercise greater diligence in the performance of my duties and increase my selling skills to become more professional." This nice, laudable statement means nothing. Sure, it sounds like a nice idea, but it isn't a clear-cut objective.

Any objective, self-development or otherwise, should be established to meet the following five criteria:

1. It must be realistic and attainable.
2. It must be measurable. (Otherwise, you don't know whether you met it.)
3. It must be clearly and unambiguously stated.
4. It must provide "stretch." (Otherwise, there's no real growth.)
5. It must be in writing.

Expert Advice: This chapter features contributions from Jim Evered.

Here are two self-development objectives that meet the above criteria:

During the next six months I will read at least three books on professional salesmanship and prepare a brief report on each for my sales manager including the key points I have applied in selling.

Within the next six months I will enroll in, and complete, a night course in marketing strategy at a local community college, and will submit to my sales manager two proposals for means of increasing our market penetration by at least 1 percent.

There are countless ways of improving on the job, but few salespeople actually do anything other than what's required by their company. Sales managers have a perfect right to expect personal development objectives from each of their salespeople on a regular and continuing basis. It is part of the manager's strategy for developing their sales personnel and bringing them to a promotable level.

Regardless of the manager's requirements, it is to the salesperson's benefit to grow in the job. There is a direct correlation between personal growth and increased earnings. It makes the sales representative more valuable to his or her customers. There is greater self-satisfaction in becoming more professional. It often gives the salesperson a big edge over the competition and produces more sales volume.

Another method of achieving self-growth is to constantly experiment with new techniques and ideas. The salesperson never lived who had the perfect way of presenting a product to a customer. A highly successful technique for one sales representative can be a complete failure for another. What one person would say to close a sale may not work at all for another. There really isn't any full explanation for it—it just happens. Differences in personality, language, communications techniques, and a host of other factors cause it. There are no 10 perfect rules for selling that will work for everyone. And for every 10 techniques you try, perhaps only one of them really works for you. This means that if you don't try all 10 of them, you will never know which one is the winner for you. You will have to try at least 100 techniques to find the 10 winners. Then you discard the 90 that didn't work and hone the other 10 to a fine edge. It is through a program of self-development that you find ideas to try, so you can separate the successful ones.

A truly professional sales representative is never satisfied with his or her selling techniques. As good as they are, there are always better ones, stronger ones, more successful ones to be found. The professional looks for them. The amateur doesn't bother. Amateurs affect everyone; they are never bad enough to fire and never good enough to promote. They clog up the pipeline of corporate growth and personal growth.

Here are some of the sources (or activities) to which a sales representative can turn to build a continuing program of self-development:

1. Libraries and bookstores for books on salesmanship, marketing, and related subjects
2. Participation in a local Toastmaster club
3. Night courses or correspondence courses at a local college or university
4. Correspondence or online courses from the American Management Association
5. Leading trade publications and magazines
6. Specialized courses periodically offered in your area, such as The Dale Carnegie Course
7. A multitude of compact disc programs on a full spectrum of job-related subjects
8. Special seminars offered on related subjects
9. Subscribing to sales publications (such as *Selling Power*)
10. In-depth discussion of selling techniques with salespeople from other industries.

There is a limitless supply of sources for growing in the job if you are really serious about it. But the key is "involvement." No one can learn for you. No one can grow for you. You must do it alone. It is your life; it is your career. Will self-improvement be part of your job description during the next 12 months? Or are you going to get the same year's experience—one more time?

ACTION STEPS

SELF-IMPROVEMENT

1. Establish and write down clear, time-specific, and measurable goals for yourself.
2. Experiment with numerous methods. The same problem may have a hundred possible solutions, and just one may work for you. Work to find it.
3. Don't ever become satisfied with what you have learned or achieved. Growth is the result of constant self-improvement.
4. Seek out new ideas in any and every place they can be found. Schools, books, seminars, and publications present a never-ending supply of new ideas you can use to achieve your dreams.

Chapter 9

Superachiever Success Traits: Do You Have What It Takes?

Objective:

To help you identify what you can do to maximize your personal potential for achievement, based on characteristics that Superachievers use to help them excel.

Synopsis:

1. Superachievers discover their true talents and convert those abilities into true proficiencies.

2. Superachievers make time work for them.

3. Superachievers perceive and seize opportunities.

4. Superachievers compensate for weaknesses through extra strength in other areas and the ability to motivate themselves.

5. Superachievers are not naturally that much better than others in their fields. They merely increase the distance between them and others through steady improvement.

In the mid-1970s, Eugene Griessman worked for an unknown entrepreneur named Ted Turner, interviewing well-known experts in literature, art, music, politics, science, religion, business, and sports. These interviews provided him with the germ for a comprehensive study of some of the most successful people in late-twentieth-century America. From home-run king Hank Aaron to publishing magnate

Malcolm Forbes to Academy Award winner Julie Andrews to former Coca-Cola Company CEO Roberto Goizueta, here's what the author of *The Achievement Factors* has to say about the paths to success of some of the most influential people of our time.

"Gradually, I became aware that two factors were always present in Superachievers," says Professor Eugene Griessman. "One, these individuals have discovered their strength; and two, they have converted that ability into a true proficiency. There is no high achievement without proficiency.

"This was true of different kinds of achievers in widely disparate fields. I began to make a list of the other themes that showed up again and again."

From entrepreneurs to baseball players to country singers, Griessman interviewed as varied a group as possible. "I wanted people who would be identified as significant by others in their field, and I chose people who I felt could explain in an articulate manner how they got where they were."

Few characteristics were universal. "You have some wide variation on what motivates people," Griessman says. "For example, musician and actor Kris Kristofferson said money was a zero when he started and that money is still a zero. Mail-order magnate Lillian Vernon Katz, on the other hand, said money was a 10 when she started and it's still a 10. But I find certain factors showing up with such frequency that I have to believe there is a causal relationship between these traits and eventual success."

Sometimes effort, not pure talent, is the real deciding factor. "Superachievers are not that much better than other top contenders in their field. They're just a little bit better. But they are a little bit better year after year after year, and like money that's left to earn interest, the interest begins to compound. Over time, that little bit grows until eventually there's a wide gap between first and second."

Superachievers also compensate for any weaknesses. He explains: "If one of these achievers is weak in an area where most Superachievers are strong, he will be very strong in another. For example, one individual might be weaker in time management than someone else, but to make up for that weakness, she will be very strong in focus."

Superachievers also share the ability to motivate themselves. This, however, does not necessarily translate into the ability to motivate others. Self-starters do not always make the best coaches.

As Griessman points out, many of the greatest managers and coaches in baseball and football history were mediocre players. "Very often successful salespeople fail when they are promoted to sales management because they have little or no training as teachers. Also, their basic personality may be perfect for selling but terrible for managing.

Bear Bryant, one of the greatest football coaches of all time, understood his strengths and defined his talent in highly specific terms. He told Griessman, "I'm not a great coach of extraordinarily talented players. I'm a good coach. I think, of that ordinary guy. I've been able to recognize those players who were not winners but didn't know it. The walls of my office are loaded down with championship pictures of people who did have the ability to win but didn't know it." Because he knew his own strengths and weaknesses, Bryant could design a team around his talents. That is what led him to great success.

People frequently ask Griessman how they too can discover their specific abilities. He answers: "One way is through intuition. Be sensitive to your own vibrations, so that you know what you respond to, and how much. As a child Martin Luther King Jr. heard powerful preachers—he saw what people could do with the spoken word, shouting, weeping, laughing. When he was six he said to his mother, 'You just wait, I'm going to get me some big words.' The same thing can happen to salespeople when they close their first sale and it turns them on. They enjoy sales. They like the contact with people and trying to solve people's problems. These are the salespeople who enjoy their work the most and, not coincidentally, are also the most successful salespeople."

How Do You Compare?

Listed below are skills, aptitudes, attitudes, experiences, and events that high achievers frequently mention as contributing to their careers.

How important have these been in your own career? (Use the following scale: 0 = low, not present, or unimportant; 10 = high, very important.)

How Important Is:
1. Time consciousness?
2. Time management?
3. Flexibility? (Being willing to alter your agenda if something important comes up)
4. Focus? (Concentrating on one thing)
5. Intensity?
6. Breadth of knowledge?
7. Competence? (Knowing or doing something very well)
8. Small details?
9. The good teacher?
10. The lucky break?
11. Being in the right place at the right time?
12. Economic incentives?
    a) At the beginning of career?
    b) Today?
13. A discoverer in your career?
14. A mentor?
15. Reading?
16. Travel?
17. Nerve?
18. Desire for recognition?
19. Feelings of inferiority?
20. Desire for self-improvement?
21. The challenge itself?
22. A sense of playfulness? Having fun?
23. Creativity?
24. Discipline?

Ask Yourself:
25. How teachable are you?
26. Are you a good listener?
27. How brave are you?

28. How persistent are you?
29. How self-confident are you?
30. How much do you enjoy your work?

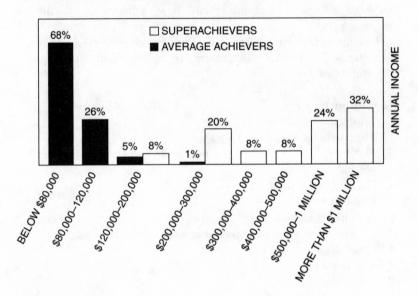

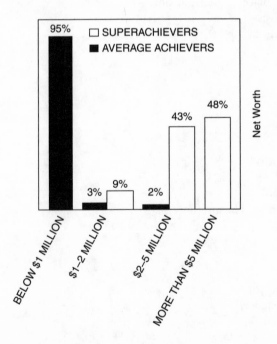

High-Achievement Factors

The factors that make for success are not career specific but are general principles of high achievement. Here, in summary, are Professor Griessman's nine "High-Achievement Factors." While these are not the only factors that lead to achievement, they are the ones mentioned again and again by the high achievers Griessman interviewed.

1. High achievers discover their vocation and their specialty. They find something they love doing, something at which they can become really proficient.
2. High achievers develop a competency. There is no long-term success without developing one's interest or specialty into a real competence.
3. High achievers value and manage time. They are aware that they live in a very time-conscious society and that they must cope with its demands.
4. High achievers are persistent. They are not easily stopped when they feel they are on the right track.
5. High achievers channel their needs and wishes into their work. They are able to channel intense desire into a focused, informed effort to realize significant goals.
6. High achievers known when and how to focus. They can tune out static and distractions to give absolute attention to the task at hand.
7. High achievers are sensitive to their environment. They recognize when they are in the right place at the right time; they understand the importance of mentors, discoverers, and teachers.
8. High achievers perceive opportunities. They are open to what is happening around them; they are always learning because they are inquisitive, questioning individuals.
9. High achievers seize opportunities. They recognize the existence and importance of trends and social forces and try to exploit them to their own benefit.

Griessman emphasizes, however, that these Superachievers were not complacent after discovering their talent. "There is always someone more talented out there. To move beyond the average achievers, these individuals cultivated their abilities to develop that talent into true proficiency. Likewise, a good salesperson works at plying his or her trade, practices closes, and studies other good salespeople. Proficiency is based on storing patterns of behavior in memory. In sales, these patterns let the salesperson know when to close, when to use a trial close, when to drop a prospect, and when to step back from the close."

As a young and admittedly second-rate car salesman, Griessman came into contact with talented and proficient salespeople. "When I was a car salesman, an older salesman told me that whenever a prospect put a hand on the car, that sign meant it was time to close. If a prospect came back from a test drive smiling—another sign that he or she was ready to buy. Car dealers learn these patterns.

"It is the same with any skill, be it acting or race car driving or drawing a comic strip. Nobel Laureate Herbert Simon said that the differentiating characteristic between an average chess player and a world-class chess player is the number of patterns each has stored in memory. A world-class chess player can recognize between 15,000 and 50,000 patterns on a chess board. To tie it all together, he said, 'I think patterns stored in memory is the basis for competence in any field.'"

Griessman says, "To become more successful than average, along with cultivating your talents to the point of proficiency, you must improve a little bit every day and you must do your very best every day. I know that sounds trite, but it's true. Earl Nightingale said that a career doesn't come to you as a career but in daily segments one day at a time. Each segment comes to you as a series of acts that you have to perform. If you perform each act as it comes to you as well as you possibly can, you are successful with that act. If you perform every act in a day that way, you've had a successful day. If you do that every day, you've had a successful life."

ACTION STEPS

SUCCESS PROFILES

1. Discover your competence.
2. Be persistent in trying to accomplish your goals.
3. Channel your intense desires into the efforts that help you realize significant goals.
4. Know when to focus; tune out distractions to give absolute attention to the task at hand.
5. Try to identify life's genuine opportunities and seize them.

PART II

UNDERSTANDING YOUR CUSTOMERS

Chapter 10

Angry Customers: Techniques for Managing Difficult Clients

Objective:

To explain the potential sources of your customers' anger and describe the best methods for placating angry customers to improve relationships.

Synopsis:

1. Anger is a natural emotion that everyone feels at one time or another.

2. Top sales performers turn their customers' anger into building blocks for better personal and business relationships.

3. One way people demonstrate anger is through silence, which can manifest itself either in the "silent treatment" or through sabotage.

4. Others openly express their anger with hostility. These people use their anger to intimidate their employees or others.

5. The "Judge" and the "Blamer" are two other angry individuals you are likely to encounter.

P icture yourself as the salesperson on the receiving end of the angry customers in these two vignettes. What would you do?

1. You obtained an order from an important customer and promised a four-week delivery. After accepting a 25 percent deposit, your production department informs your customer—but

not you!—that the model on order is no longer available. Unknowingly, you visit your customer and he confronts you with an expression of anger and disbelief.

2. You sold a business machine to a law firm. One week after their office personnel have been trained in the use of your equipment, the client learns that they could have purchased a similar competitive model for 20 percent less. The lawyer calls you and accuses you of deceptive business practices.

Anger in customers is perplexing. If it's unmanaged, you're going to lose valuable customers, find it difficult working with employees, and get in dutch with the boss. Anger always is expressed—whether outwardly or inwardly. Often it's covert and indirect. Coming late, absenteeism, and losing things around the office are examples of covert expressions of hostility. Blowing up, confronting people with negative feelings, and blaming people are more overt expressions of anger. Anger is something that can either get in your way or be managed in such a way as to expedite your work and get your job done.

Anger is not sinful, weird, sick, or crazy. Anger is a natural, normal emotion that all human beings have, and we all have the opportunity to learn to deal with it. Look at it this way. You either control your anger or your anger controls you. Successful people are those who acknowledge their emotions—even the difficult ones like anger—and learn how to express them appropriately.

Look at the two vignettes above. How would you have handled those kinds of situations? Do you feel equipped to deal with the emotional impact aroused either in yourself or in other people by the examples given? When you manage your client's anger there are a number of benefits. You release the tension in the situation. You open communication. You unblock the energy needed for clear thinking. In addition, learning to handle your client's anger will give

Expert Advice: This chapter features contributions from Robert W. Cromey.

you a chance to build a closer relationship. It's not unusual that an initial conflict once successfully managed makes room for a long-lasting and profitable business relationship. It's a truism in psychology that a mutual emotional investment creates a lasting bond.

SILENT ANGER

There are many styles of expressing anger. We can deal with them under two categories. One is the silent treatment, or the flight response. This is a way to get away from dealing with the anger and hostility that you feel. You go inside yourself and retreat and withdraw—in fact, the silent treatment as we experience it is that people literally do not speak to the person they're mad at. This often happens in marriages, and very often happens around an office.

Another form of the silent treatment is sabotage, crime, and obstructionism in the workplace. I heard of a company that every day for three months had to call a plumber because somebody went into the men's room and stuffed two rolls of toilet paper down into the toilet, causing it to overflow. Obviously the person was expressing anger covertly and silently and effectively. I'm sure you can think of examples in your own workplace of this particular way of expressing anger.

EXPLOSIONS

The second category for expressing anger is what can be called open anger. The most obvious example is the exploder. This person shouts and screams and hollers whenever he gets angry. This person is usually somebody in charge or who has power and uses it to intimidate employees and salespeople who approach him. It can be used as a manipulative technique to keep people off balance. It's not a very direct or fair way to work with people.

TIPS

4 Tips for Dealing with Angry Customers

1   Share the anger. Hear out your angry customers without cutting them off or belittling their feelings.

2   Empathize. Use a situation from your life that compares with what your customer is feeling.

3   Reassure your clients. Let them know that if they can see beyond the current problem, the potential for a better relationship will grow.

4   Stay calm and ask questions. Think of questions that will uncover hidden misunderstandings, current difficulties, or false rumors they may have heard about you or your company.

Then there's what I call the John Wayne approach to expressing anger: revenge. The old saying goes, "I don't get angry—I get even." Around the office it goes like this: "Next time you do this, I'm going to fire you."

Another example of expressing anger is the judge: a person going around passing judgments on other people's behavior. "It's not fair when you talk to me like this."

Then there's the blamer. That person usually starts sentences with, "You should have . . ." or "I told you . . .", implying somehow that you are bad and wrong for whatever you've done. Instead of being direct and saying, "I'm angry" or "I'm upset," the attempt is to put the blame on the other person. The nitpicker can also be a person who is expressing anger. Challenging the budget and constantly complaining about little details can be a means of expressing hostility under the guise of being a super performer.

DISARMING THE HOSTILE CUSTOMER

When I was national sales manager of a middle-size consumer product company, I called on a major account we had lost. Our local sales representative had set up the appointment for me.

When I walked in, it was a hostile situation from the very start. Hanging on the firm's wall was a letter from our company's old credit manager. It was nasty, indignant, and insulting to our prospect. To top it off, that old credit manager was now our company's general manager and my boss.

Thus, when I began my sales pitch, there were many strikes against me. But all of a sudden I found the vehicle that would both disarm my prospect and get him to listen to me. Two "Batakas" were in the corner of the room. "Batakas" are padded aggression bats used in martial encounters and group therapy sessions. They are usually owned by aggressive people who need a physical outlet without hurting others.

I knew I was getting nowhere with the owner of this company, so I blurted out: "You want to fight?" He answered, "Yes." So we went at it with the "Batakas" in hand. After five minutes of grueling combat in coats and suits, my adversary won. Of course, he felt a lot better.

He sat down and wrote one of the largest orders my company had ever seen!

The moral of this story: Don't be afraid to take a risk and do what some would say is foolish. Be willing to do the outlandish to get the order. The buyer might even turn out to become your best friend.

by Joseph A. Perthes, Performance Marketing Associates, Northridge, California

ANGER MANAGEMENT TECHNIQUES

Here are some key rules for managing people who are angry and upset:

Don't try to control or threaten people who are angry. You can't control another person's anger; you can show that you are understanding. A good way to do this is just to allow them to be angry without criticizing or somehow trying to get them to stop expressing their anger. Give them some time to share their anger and talk about it.

Show understanding about how your client feels. For example, you can say something like, "I understand how you feel, and I see that getting what you ordered is a major concern at this time. I'd be angry too if that happened to me." It's probably best to stay with allowing the customer to express his anger and not be tempted to say something like, "You're right, our production department is making a big mistake in discontinuing the model. It's infuriating, I know." In-house criticism is not going to be very helpful to the people involved. Stick with the feeling of anger and stick with allowing the person to have the anger until you can calm him or her down and begin to renegotiate the situation.

A third key rule for handling angry customers is to assure the client that the anger won't jeopardize the relationship. For example, you can say, "I understand your reaction and appreciate your openness. You see this gives me a chance to work harder to make our relationship work." Or you can say something like, "I'm sure you realize your business is very important to me."

Then, after your clients have had time to vent their anger, you can clarify, diagnose, and respond to the real issues. "Now, could you help me understand the details of this competitive offer?" Once you've allowed the venting of angry feelings, you can begin to think through what the problem is and see if some new answers can be established. This is a time when you can renegotiate and build new bridges in the relationship. This is very difficult to do if the person has not had a chance to get any of his angry feelings put forward. Any attempts on your part to block those feelings because of fear or anxiety will get in the way of your continuing the relationship and bridging on to new business.

Watch out for the nonverbal expressions of anger. It's a good idea not to mirror the client's negative, nonverbal expressions. Don't withdraw, don't show defensiveness; express an open posture. Look at the person without challenge, but with caring. Crossing your legs and arms will only show a desire to retreat on your part and make it more difficult to establish communication with your customer.

MANAGING THE SILENT CUSTOMER

When you encounter a customer who is obviously upset and angry but is also silent, you have a big problem. You can tell the person is annoyed by his clenched, jaw, averted glance, and unwillingness to communicate very openly or directly. The problem is difficult for you because you don't have any information. You don't know what the problem is and it seems embarrassing or too personal to ask. The customer is in the passive manipulating position and can create feelings in you of self-doubt and insecurity.

Here are some key strategies that could help. You can answer questions that are essentially statements about the customer's silence:

- "Is there anything about me or my company that prevents you from doing business with us?"
- "I can't help noticing that 1 have been doing most of the talking, and at this point I'd like to ask you what seems to hold you back from expressing your objective opinion."
- "Obviously, you must have a reason for saving your objective opinion on what we've been discussing. Would you mind if I asked what it is?"

If you use these techniques, be prepared to accept open anger. You may push a button that will help the person express his anger and hostility directly. Then you can revert to the strategies mentioned above of listening and allowing the person to vent his anger, and then sit down with him to discuss and renegotiate your situation.

In summary, you can manage other people's anger. It takes a certain amount of derring-do, but not really all that much. Be prepared to listen, ask searching questions, and be willing to take the risk of confronting anger directly. It's important to remember that anger is okay. It is there to be handled, and it can be something with which you can be enormously creative.

Finally, in dealing with other people's anger you will learn something about your own. The best management technique for handling angry clients is to improve your own anger management skills. The more comfortable you are with your own anger and hostility, the better chance you have of effectively defusing a client's anger and turning it into a creative selling opportunity.

ACTION STEPS

ANGRY CUSTOMERS

1. Don't try to control or threaten an angry customer.
2. Try to let them know that you care about their anger.
3. Assure the angry customer that you won't let his or her anger jeopardize your relationship.
4. If you suspect that a silent customer is angry, try, with caution, to elicit the source of the anger.
5. Be prepared to absorb the brunt of your customers' anger or you will never move beyond the anger to grow the relationship.

Chapter 11

Confrontation: Make Problems Work for You

Objective:

To teach you how to utilize a method of "constructive criticism" to make confrontational situations work for you, rather than against you.

Synopsis:

1. Because most people fear direct confrontation, many business problems are never resolved.

2. "Constructive confrontation" is a method of addressing differences of opinion openly without allowing personal hostility to enter into the discussion.

3. Constructive confrontation accelerates problem solving by encouraging people to concentrate on solving problems, not finding scapegoats.

4. Confrontation and the resultant solutions to problems represent the essence of corporate health.

5. Constructive confrontation does not mean being loud, unpleasant, or rude, and it is not designed to affix blame.

In looking for new ways to build relationships with customers, I asked Andrew S. Grove, former CEO and current senior advisor at Intel, his techniques for learning from confrontation. The rest of this chapter provides his winning technique of constructive confrontation.

* * *

Most people avoid confrontation. Managers don't give meaningful performance evaluations because they are afraid to say what they really think or fear an angry response. Coworkers ignore a problem or carry around destructive resentment rather than confront a difficult situation head-on. Problems get worse, bad feelings run rampant, and both employees and their companies suffer.

At Intel, we developed a direct approach to problem solving that eliminates this destructive pattern. We call it "constructive confrontation."

WHY HAVE CONSTRUCTIVE CONFRONTATION?

Everybody knows that problems are inevitable in business. Machines stop working properly. Orders are lost to the competition; coworkers don't perform their tasks the way we think they should. Such problems often produce conflicts.

If an order was lost, was it because the salesperson goofed or because product quality has slipped? Members of the sales force and quality-control people will probably disagree on the cause. But if the company is to get the customer back, it must find the right answer to the question and solve the problem.

Constructive confrontation accelerates problem solving. Participants must be direct and deal with people face-to-face—as soon as possible—to keep the problem from festering. And it encourages

---

Expert Advice: This chapter features contributions from Andrew S. Grove, the former Chairman and CEO of the Board of Intel Corporation. He currently serves as senior advisor for Intel, among other companies. In 1997, he was named *Time* magazine's Man of the Year.

everyone to concentrate on the problem, not on the people caught up in it.

Many managers seem to think it is impolite to tackle anything or anyone, even in business. Actually, it is the essence of corporate health to bring a problem out into the open right away, even if this entails a confrontation. Workplace politicking grows quietly in the dark. It is like a mushroom; neither can stand the light of day.

FIGHTING IT OUT SAVES TIME

I learned my lesson while I was a relatively young and inexperienced manager. I let myself get sucked into the middle of some unproductive political infighting. Two of my subordinates, one in charge of manufacturing and the other of quality assurance, came to dislike each other. The manufacturing manager would walk into my office and complain to me that the quality manager didn't know what he was doing. Ten minutes later, the quality manager would tell me that his counterpart disregarded procedures, that he didn't give a hoot about quality.

I found myself investigating first one small claim and then another, getting more and more anxious and angry. Finally I decided I would not tolerate it anymore. The next time one of them began the routine, I raised my hand and stopped him. "Hold it," I said. "Let's get the other person in here." When he appeared, I said to the first manager in my office: "Now tell me what you were going to say." The confrontation between the two was tense and embarrassing—anything but constructive. But after a few such sessions, both managers discovered that dealing directly with each other was a lot less awkward and more productive than a scene in my office.

ATTACKING THE PROBLEM, NOT THE PERSON

Constructive confrontation does not mean being loud, unpleasant, or rude, and it is not designed to affix blame. It means attacking a problem by speaking up in a businesslike way. Say that you are in a meeting. The man across the table is droning on with a clearly unworkable idea. When you are sure you understand his point, interrupt him politely: "I disagree with your proposed solution. It won't work because . . ." Attack the problem, not the individual.

If you find yourself saying, "You're out of your mind to even suggest such a thing," you're doing it wrong. Indeed, as long as the focus of what you say is the individual, even the most delicate phrasing won't help much. A remark like, "With all due respect, I can't help but wonder what you might have been thinking of when you came up with this plan," while exquisite in its politeness, still misses the target. When you do focus correctly—on the problem—never be rude. Saying, "The solution you propose is absurd" isn't constructive confrontation either.

Admittedly, this system is hard to practice. While a few people are natural "black belts' at the technique, most find it somewhat painful, at least initially, because they have been brought up to think that politeness excludes confrontation. People who have trouble picking up the technique should be comforted by the fact that they're in good company. Consider the following, from a column by Joseph Kraft: "Ronald Reagan enjoyed a reputation as a fierce tiger in asserting American interests. But foreign leaders repeatedly came away from sessions with the former President claiming he is a pussycat—too nice even to mention disagreeable subjects."

DON'T BULLDOZE YOUR CLIENTS

The practice of constructive confrontation has to be managed, of course, particularly with people outside the company. At Intel, we learned not to impose our style of direct problem solving on others unfamiliar with it—like customers. Once, I paid a sales call on one of our largest customers, a company known for its indirect and non-confrontational internal style. Accompanied by a group of sales and marketing people, I participated in a fairly large meeting, which included some of the senior management of the other company.

We ran into a few problems and went to work on them. The discussion meandered around far too long compared with what I was accustomed to at Intel. Without even realizing what I was doing, I started to take over the meeting—asking questions, directing the discussion. Nobody objected, so I thought nothing of it until we left.

Once we were outside the customer's building, the Intel salespeople gathered around and almost lynched me for behavior they considered totally inappropriate in the customer's presence. They were correct. The story of that meeting reverberated through the other company. Our salespeople had to make a number of follow-up visits to smooth the feathers I had ruffled.

Sometimes, of course, a situation simply runs away from us. Rational arguments give way to a scene in which the participants need to win an argument much more than they need to resolve an issue. When that happens, it's best to adjourn the confrontation. When things aren't getting anywhere, raise your hand and say, "Hold it! Let's take this up later when everybody is cooler." When you reconvene, chances are that all present will be thinking more clearly. Then they will be ready for the kind of confrontation that works.

ACTION STEPS

CONFRONTATION

1. Attack the problem, not the individual. Disagree, for example, with the solution, not the solution's sponsor.
2. Don't ever be rude. Disagree politely. If you say, "That solution is absurd!" you are not confronting constructively.
3. Don't use constructive criticisms on people—especially customers—who may not understand that you are just trying to solve problems. Better to let them dictate the tone of discussion.
4. If and when a situation gets out of hand, it is best to adjourn the meeting until cooler heads can prevail.

Chapter 12

Customer Types: Selling to Different Personalities

Objective:

To examine the four main customer types and ways you can adapt your personal style to sell most effectively to each of them.

Synopsis:

1. Many sales that appear difficult only seem so because the customer's buying style does not match your selling style.

2. Based on whether customers are open or self-contained and whether they manage information directly or indirectly, you can determine whether they are Relaters, Thinkers, Socializers, or Directors.

   a) Relaters are open and manage information indirectly.

   b) Thinkers are self-contained and manage information indirectly.

   c) Socializers are open and manage information directly.

   d) Directors are self-contained and manage information directly.

We've all had our share of easy sales and, unfortunately, more than our share of tough ones. Remember those easy sales that you made? It seemed that everything went right, especially the ease with which you built trust and rapport with those customers. You could do no wrong. In fact, a few of your easy sales were actually tough ones for some of your fellow salespeople.

The tough sales are the ones you want to forget. As hard and as long as you worked on them, nothing seemed to come together. You just couldn't get on the same wavelength as your "tough" prospects and some you couldn't sell at all. They seemed to turn you off. It was like there was some hidden barrier between you and those tough prospects that made it very difficult, and even impossible, to sell them.

Many of your tough prospects aren't really tough at all. They're only tough for you because your selling style does not match their personality style. That's why other salespeople with a different selling style than your own find it much easier to sell your tough prospects. Their selling style matches the personality style of your tough prospects.

But just how do you change your selling style so that it is "right" for your difficult prospects? And how can you know as early as possible in the sales presentation which prospects will be the tough ones for you? Finally, how can you actually close many more of your tough prospects than you are closing right now?

HOW DO YOUR CUSTOMERS WANT TO BE SOLD?

A crucial skill in building trust is the ability to form accurate impressions of your prospects. This requires interpreting a

Expert Advice: This chapter features contributions from Jim Cathcart and Dr. Anthony Alessandra. Cathcart's company, Cathcart Institute, Inc., is a research and education resource for executives and salespeople who want to take personal initiative to make their organizations and communities better (www.cathcart.com). Alessandra is the president of Online Assessments (www.OnlineAC.com), a company that offers online assessments and tests to help companies build customers, relationships, and the bottom-line (www.alessandra.com).

prospect's individual style, noting those signals that indicate how the prospect would like to be treated by you. You can begin classifying your customers' behavior by observing how they manage themselves and how they manage information:

A. How customers manage themselves

Open behavior. Is your customer ready and willing to show emotions or feelings? Open behavior signals describe a person as being relaxed, warm, responsive, informal, and personable. Customers displaying open behavior need to be flexible about time, share their personal feelings, and like to tell stories and anecdotes.

Self-contained behavior. Is your customer formal and proper, reluctant to show emotions and feelings? Self-contained behavior signals describe a person as being guarded and aloof. Customers displaying self-contained behavior tend to base their decisions on cold, hard facts. They tend to be disciplined about time and are task-oriented.

B. How customers manage information

Indirect. Does your customer avoid control and involvement? Customers who manage information indirectly come across as quiet, shy, and reserved. They tend to move slowly, meditate on their decisions, and avoid risks. They tend to be supportive and listen more than they talk. They often reserve their opinions and make tentative statements.

Direct. Does your customer exercise a great deal of control over the information presented? Customers who manage information directly tend to come on strong, take the social initiative, and create a powerful first impression. They tend to be fast-paced people who make swift decisions and like to take risks. They often become impatient with others who cannot keep up with their fast pace. They do a lot of talking, express their opinions readily, and appear confident.

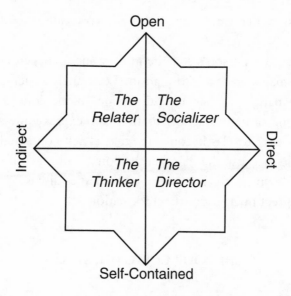

A TYPICAL EXAMPLE

I recall a client with whom I eventually had a highly successful sales relationship. My first appointment was made by her secretary for 10:10 a.m. (not 10:00 a.m. or 10:30 a.m.). As I arrived a few minutes early, the secretary had me sit in the reception area. My future client came out of her office, acknowledged my presence with a polite "canned" smile, and gave a list of detailed instructions to the secretary. I noticed she was meticulously dressed.

With another polite smile, she asked me to follow her into the office. She told me where to sit, looked at her watch, phoned her secretary to hold all calls for 15 minutes, hung up, looked at her watch again, and said, "You have 15 minutes. Go!"

During my presentation, this client remained as quiet and expressionless as a statue on Mount Rushmore. No emotion showed. She asked for specific details, assessed the responses, and extended the discussion. She actually did the confirming, invited me to stay longer, and fully settled the sale after specific responses to her time, schedule, and cost questions had been answered.

Clues to this person's style lie in how she managed herself and how she managed the information. Let's analyze her behavioral style. By nature of her time-discipline, meticulous dress, task orientation, formality, fact orientation, and expressionless face, she was fairly easy to classify on one scale as self-contained. On the other scale, because she directed the conversation, confronted the issues, and controlled and confirmed the issues discussed, she came out as a direct manager of the information.

THE FOUR CUSTOMER STYLES

When both scales are combined, they form four quadrants that identify different and recognizable customer styles. These are the Socializer, the Director, the Thinker, and the Relater.

Each quadrant represents unique combinations of self-management and information management and is linked to separate and unique ways of behaving with salespeople. The name given to each style reflects a very general characteristic rather than a full or accurate description. As you better understand why customers behave the way they do, your knowledge can help you communicate effectively and openly in a way that helps them feel more comfortable in their interactions with you. Throughout this chapter, you will find guidelines on how to best match your selling style to your customer's individual style.

NO BEST STYLE

Each style has its own unique strengths and weaknesses, and successful people as well as failures populate each style group. There is no "best" behavioral style.

Customers possess traits from all four styles in varying degrees. Depending on circumstances, one style may be more dominant than any of the others. However, most people do have a single dominant behavioral style. In selling, it is very important always to be aware of the style that your prospect or customer is exhibiting on each and every call. In order to increase your sales success, you need to accurately identify their individual styles and respond accordingly. Let's see how it's done.

THE RELATER

The Relater Style. The Relater manages information in indirect ways and shows open behavior. Relaters tend to be relatively unassertive, warm, supportive, and reliable. They are sometimes seen by others as compliant and soft-hearted. Relaters seek security and belongingness and are slow at taking action and making decisions. Before they take any action or make a decision, they have to know how other people feel about it. Relaters dislike interpersonal conflicts so much that they sometimes say what they think other people want to hear rather than what is really on their minds. Relaters have tremendous counseling skills and are extremely supportive of other people. They are also incredibly active listeners. You usually feel good by just being with a Relater.

How to sell to the Relater. Try to support the Relater's feelings and project that you are interested in him or her as a person. Move along in an informal, slow manner, and constantly show the Relater that you are actively listening. Discuss personal opinions and feelings. Try to explore potential areas for future misunderstanding or dissatisfaction. The Relater likes guarantees that any new actions will involve a minimum risk. Therefore, offer personal assurances of support. Try not to rush the Relater, but do provide guidance. Project genuine sincerity in your relationship.

- Plan to get to know them personally. Be likeable and non-threatening, professional but friendly.
- Meet them by developing trust, friendship, and credibility. Go at a slow pace.
- Study their feelings and emotional needs as well as their technical and business needs.
- Propose by getting them involved. Show the human side of your proposal.
- Confirm without pushing or rushing them. Provide personal assurances and guarantees wherever you can.
- Assure by being consistent in your communication. Give them the nurturing and reassurance that you would give someone who was highly concerned about the purchase they had just made.

THE SOCIALIZER

The Socializer Style. The Socializer manages information directly and shows open behavior. He readily exhibits characteristics such as animation, intuitiveness, and liveliness. The Socializer is an idea person—a dreamer, a fast-paced person with spontaneous actions and decisions and a lack of concern for facts or details. This disregard for details sometimes prompts him or her to exaggerate and generalize facts and figures.

Socializers are more comfortable with "best guesstimates" than with hard researched facts. They thrive on involvement with others and tend to work quickly and enthusiastically with others. They often seek approval and pats on the back for their accomplishments and achievements. Socializers always love an audience. They are very creative and think quickly on their feet.

How to sell to the Socializer. The Socializer likes to interact with other people, so try not to hurry the discussion. Attempt to develop some mutually stimulating ideas together. Focus your conversation on opinions, ideas, and dreams, and then try to support them.

Make sure you try to move at a pace that is both entertaining and fast-moving. Instead of arguing, try to explore alternative solutions you both can share with enthusiasm.

When you finally reach an agreement, iron out the specific details concerning what, when, who, and how. Summarize in writing what you both agreed upon, even though it may not appear necessary. Finally, make sure you are both in full agreement concerning when actions are to be performed.

- Plan to be stimulating and interested in them. Allow them time to talk.
- Meet them boldly; don't be shy. Introduce yourself first. Bring up new topics openly.
- Study their dreams and goals as well as their other needs.
- Propose your solution with stories or illustrations that relate to them and their goals.
- Confirm the details in writing. Be clear and direct.
- Ensure that they fully understand what they bought and can demonstrate their ability to use it properly.

THE THINKER

The Thinker Style. The Thinker manages information indirectly and communicates self-contained behavior. Thinkers seem to be very concerned with thought processes and are persistent, systematic problem solvers. They can also be seen as aloof, picky, and critical. Thinkers are very security conscious and have a high need to be right. This leads them to overreliance on data collection. In their quest for data, they tend to ask many questions about specific details. Their actions and decisions tend to be extremely cautious.

Thinkers work slowly and precisely by themselves and prefer an intellectual work environment that is organized and structured. They tend to be skeptical and like to see things in writing. (This comes across as a "show me" attitude.) Although they are great problem solvers, Thinkers are poor decision makers.

How to sell to the Thinker. Try to be systematic, exact, organized, and prepared with the Thinker. Try to support the Thinker's organized, thoughtful approach. Thinkers may require that you send them solid, tangible, factual evidence that what you say is true and accurate. List the advantages and disadvantages of any plan you propose to the Thinker and have viable alternatives for dealing effectively with the disadvantages. If you do not bring up the obvious disadvantages in your product or plan, the Thinker will certainly find them out. Try not to rush the decision-making process with Thinkers because they need time to verify your words and your actions.

- Plan to be well prepared and equipped to answer all their questions.
- Meet them cordially but get quickly to the task.
- Study their situation in a practical, logical manner. Make sure your questions show a clear direction.
- Propose logical solutions to their problems. Document the how and the why and show how your proposition is the logical thing to do.
- Confirm as a matter of course. Don't push; give them time to think. Offer documentation.
- Assure them with excellent service and follow through. Be complete.

THE DIRECTOR

The Director Style. The Director manages information directly and at the same time displays self-contained behavior. Directors exhibit firmness in their relationship with others and are oriented toward productivity and bottom-line results. Closely allied to these positive traits are the negative ones of stubbornness, impatience, and toughness. Directors tend to take control of other people and situations and are decisive in both their actions and their decisions. They like to move at an extremely fast pace and are very impatient with delays. They seem to want things yesterday.

Directors are high achievers and exhibit very good administrative skills. They certainly get things done and make things happen. Directors like to do many things at the same time. Because of their high-achievement motivation, they show a tendency toward work-aholism.

How to sell to the Director. Directors are easy to deal with so long as you are precise, efficient, disciplined, and organized. Make sure you keep your relationship businesslike. Do not attempt to establish a personal relationship unless that is one of the Director's objectives. Focus your conversation around the Director's goals. If during the conversation you must take issue with the Director, argue the facts, not personal feelings. Make sure you can back up your facts with solid, tangible proof.

You should provide the Director with options. Directors like to make their own decisions.

- Plan to be prepared and organized, fast paced, and to the point.
- Meet them in such a way that you get to the point quickly; keep things professional and businesslike.
- Study their goals and objectives.
- Propose solutions with clearly defined consequences and rewards that relate specifically to the Director's goals.
- Confirm, provide two to three options, and let the Director make the decision.
- Assure them that their time will not be wasted. After the sale, confirm that the proposals you suggested did in fact provide the bottom-line results expected.

ACTION STEPS

CUSTOMER TYPES

1. To sell to the Relater, be personable, develop credibility slowly, and give constant reassurance.
2. To sell to the Thinker, be systematic, organized, cordial, and logical. Explain advantages and disadvantages clearly with explanations for dealing with the disadvantages.
3. To sell to the Socializer, try to brainstorm mutually agreeable solutions together. When you do hammer out a solution, write down the details and make sure you agree on how to proceed.
4. To sell to the Director, be precise, noncontrolling, and factual. Provide options for the Director to choose from.

Chapter 13

Lies & Deception: How to Deal with Dishonesty in Selling

Objective:

To explain ways you can read the subtle clues your customers—and others—give away to expose whether they are telling you the truth.

Synopsis:

1. Although most people give off distinct clues when they are lying, few of us are capable of identifying lies with any consistency.

2. When, in social situations, we don't share our true feelings out of courtesy, we should not consider ourselves liars.

3. When a person experiences true enjoyment, the muscles that circle the eyes deepen. If they do not deepen while the customer smiles, the smile may be fake.

4. People are less capable of controlling body language than words.

Although most people think that they are very good at catching liars, Dr. Paul Ekman's latest research reveals that unless you are a Secret Service agent, your ability to spot lies is just about as good as flipping a coin. In a research project at the University of California, more than 500 men and women, including police detectives, psychiatrists, judges, polygraph testers, and Secret Service agents, were tested on their ability to assess whether a person was lying or telling the truth. Surprisingly, only the Secret Service agents did better than chance on catching the liars. "The problem is," says Dr. Ekman, "most people will never know that they have been lied to and we are not very good at reading lies because we don't expect them." Dr. Ekman has taught psychiatrists, judges, lawyers, and government officials to improve their ability to spot lies. After his workshop, participants' lie-catching scores usually improve from 50 percent to over 80 percent. This chapter is based on an exclusive interview with Dr. Paul Ekman, who shares his latest research that can help you uncover the nonverbal clues to deception. He also discusses practical strategies for getting the truth to the surface in selling situations and during job interviews.

A QUESTION OF LIFE AND DEATH

"As I worked on the problem," explains Dr. Ekman, "I came to see that there are lies in every area of life and remarkably little was known about deception and behavioral clues to deceit."

TAKING PEOPLE FOR A RIDE

After important negotiations with business leaders in his high-rise office building, John D. Rockefeller used to say goodbye to his visitors at the elevator. While the group filed into the elevator, an inno-cent-looking man slipped in and rode with them to the ground floor. He would follow the group out the door and then cross the street. A few minutes later, the young man went back to Rockefeller's office to deliver a detailed report of what the unsuspecting visitors talked about during the ride in the elevator.

THE TWO BASIC FORMS OF LYING

In his book *Telling Lies,* Dr. Ekman writes: "There are two primary ways to lie: to conceal and to falsify. In concealing, the liar withholds some information without actually saying anything untrue. In falsifying, the liar takes an additional step. Not only does the liar withhold true information, but he presents false information as if it were true."

Are there situations when deception is not considered as a lie? What about when a dear relative gives you something that you don't really like for Christmas? Do you tell the truth, or do you say, "Thanks for the thoughtful gift"? Dr. Ekman would not call that a lie, because "in social situations there is a mutual expectation that we will treat one another politely. There is a mutual expectation that we will act in a civil fashion and be considerate of each other's feelings. That kind of deception should not be considered as lying."

While politeness is part of a social ritual that does not always demand the truth, sometimes people insist that the truth be told. Dr. Ekman recalled one day when his wife came home with a new dress and asked him how he liked it. After he answered, "Honey, that's really smashing and you look great," his wife asked again, this time with a tone of uncertainty, "No, really, tell me the truth, is it really right for me or not?" Given the license to tell her what he really thought, he added, "Now that you mention it, it may be a bit too flashy for you."

HOW SMILES COVER TRUE EMOTIONS

The drawback with polite conversation is that people never know how others really feel. The most common way to conceal any strong emotion is to smile. How can we tell when a customer's smile is not an expression of true enjoyment? Dr. Ekman, who has studied facial expressions among people in the United States,

Europe, Russia, and Japan, explains the subtle clues that tell the difference: "When people experience real enjoyment, the muscles that circle the eyes are involved in the smile. In a slight smile it is very easy to notice the contraction of the muscles around the eyes. If it is a very broad smile, then the signs become more subtle and you can't look at the cheeks or the crow's feet to get an accurate reading. You have to look at the skin above the eye. If the broad smile is a true enjoyment smile, the skin above the eye will come down a little, and the eyelids are slightly lower. This is the kind of smile that accompanies the changes in the brain that occur with enjoyment."

According to Dr. Ekman's research, polite smiles often let other people know that we agree with what they are doing or saying. Sometimes salespeople put on a smile to show how much they are enjoying a customer's amusing story when they actually think that it is boring. These smiles serve to facilitate rapport and can't be considered as false smiles.

Why would we want to know when a customer's smile is real or a polite mask? During product demonstrations, it pays to know exactly what product features the customer really likes. When the customer's smile deepens the crow's feet around the eyes, it may be the best time to ask for the order.

IT'S HARD TO LOOK COOL WHEN WE'RE HOT

While it is easy to fake a smile, negative emotions are much harder to falsify. The hardest thing to do is look cool when you feel real, strong emotions. It also takes great effort to falsify feelings of distress and fear, while expressions of anger or disgust are relatively simple to counterfeit.

Since emotions are expressed more clearly through body language, Dr. Ekman suggests paying close attention to such nonverbal communication channels as face, tone of voice, and body.

Scientific research confirms that when people focus only on words, they often miss critical information. "Everyone knows that when we use words, we can say whatever we want and easily conceal the truth," says Dr. Ekman, "but it takes extraordinary skills to deceive the trained eye with our face, voice, and body."

For example, 70 percent of the people studied involuntarily raise the pitch of their voice when they get upset. Although some people raise the pitch when they are lying, Dr. Ekman warns against misinterpretations. "A raised pitch does not automatically indicate deception. Most of the time it only indicates the presence of fear, excitement, or anger."

He also warns about misinterpreting a low, flat, and unemotional tone of voice. It is possible for a gifted performer to deliver an emotionally charged story calmly and evenly. During the Watergate hearings, John Dean testified that President Nixon had approved payoffs. Years after his testimony, John Dean revealed in his book *Blind Ambition* that he had decided in advance to "read

---

HOW DIFFERENT CULTURES JUSTIFY LYING

Every country follows its own rules for deception:

Russia: Lie, but don't overdo it.

Denmark: To find credence, lies must be patched with truth.

Germany: A necessary lie is harmless.

Sweden: A lie in time of need is as good as the truth.

Romania: A well-turned lie pays better than the truth.

Czech Republic: Better a lie that heals than a truth that wounds.

evenly, unemotionally, and as coldly as possible and answer questions the same way." Dean reasoned that "people tend to think that somebody telling the truth will be calm about it." Judge John J. Sirica appeared to be impressed with John Dean's unemotional tone of voice, as he indicated in his book *To Set The Record Straight*: "The committee members peppered him with hostile questions. But he stuck to his story. He didn't appear upset in any way. His flat, unemotional tone of voice made him believable."

HOW TO CHECK IF PEOPLE ARE LYING

What makes it so hard to catch a liar is that many people end up believing their own lies. In many instances, people explain a situation to themselves, then edit their account to their liking until they have fabricated an acceptable story that interweaves reality and fiction. Through the process of repeating the same story over and over, the storyteller assumes ownership of the new account. How would a professional lie catcher separate fact from fiction in a situation like a job interview, an important business negotiation, or a major sale?

HOW TO GET THE TRUTH TO SURFACE

What if you sense that someone may not be telling the truth? How do you obtain accurate information without antagonizing the other person and without leaving the door open to further lies?

Dr. Ekman suggests not putting people on the defensive: "Show them that you really want to build a bridge and encourage them to be frank." He also suggests being sensitive to the other person: "Most of us don't like to admit to ourselves that we are lying. And whenever we do lie, we tend to think that we have a very good justification."

The Classic Lies Customers Will Use on You

When prospects fail to recognize the benefits of buying, they are often too embarrassed to tell the truth. Instead of taking the time to objectively investigate the opportunity you are presenting, they seek an immediate shortcut by fabricating a small lie. Although any of the statements below sound true, and can be true, you will never know if they really are unless you probe further to isolate the true reason behind your prospect's shortcut. The most common lies in selling follow the 10 distinct patterns listed below:

1. *Denial*
   "I don't need this new product."
   "I would not think of trading in my old machine."
   "There is no reason for changing now."
2. *Alibi*
   "I don't have the money to buy."
   "I don't have the authority."
3. *Blaming*
   "It's not my responsibility to make that decision."
   "My boss does not like products like that."
   "I want it, but my husband (wife) doesn't like it."
4. *Minimizing*
   "This new idea won't do us much good."
   "I don't see what's so great about this."
   "There is little value to spending money on this."
5. *Justification*
   "We do have a need, but we are too busy with our reorganization."
   "I would like to go ahead right now, but the budget hasn't been approved."
   "It's no use. As long as business is slow, we can't spend money."
6. *Derogation*
   "I heard that these things suffer from frequent breakdowns."
   "When it comes to service, nobody will be around to help us."
   "You don't have a good reputation in this area."
   "It's a good idea, but it won't work here."
7. *Cost*
   "Yes, it is inexpensive, but we can't afford it."
   "We'd like to buy two, but not right now."
8. *Helplessness*
   "It's out of my hands. I can't do this deal."
   "If I could convince my boss, I'd buy it today."
   "There is no way my wife would agree to that."

9. *I have no choice*

"I tried my best, but I had no choice but to go along with the majority."

"With the many problems we've had in the past, I had no choice but to cancel the order."

"Based on the lower offer that we've received from your competitor, I had no choice but to go with them."

10. *Reframing reality*

"Robin Hood was not stealing. He just redistributed the wealth."

"Our purchasing system is not unfair. We are just limiting the number of suppliers."

"We may have caused you a minor inconvenience by canceling this order, but believe me, we are saving you a lot of money in the future, because your product would have had a lot of service problems with this type of application."

Why isn't it a good strategy to call someone a liar? Simply because the moment you turn the relationship into an adversarial situation, people may refuse to talk with you further. If you depend on

TIPS

6 TIPS FOR CATCHING LIES DURING JOB INTERVIEWS

1 Prepare good interview questions.

2 Ask follow-up questions and probe for finer details.

3 Listen with your eyes and ears.

4 Develop a list of inconsistencies and possible lies.

5 Schedule a second interview. Prepare finely tuned follow-up questions.

6 Plan a third interview with a different interviewer and compare notes.

additional information from that particular source, you may be giving up your advantage. "In most instances," explains Dr. Ekman, "people will feel more comfortable if you can reassure them that they are not going to risk a lot if they tell you the truth."

How can we reassure other people that they won't lose everything if they tell us the truth? Here are a few ways to get people to relax:

- "Perhaps there is some reason why you can't share with me what really happened."
- "Are you worried about how I might react to what you are telling me?"
- "I know that this may be uncomfortable, but it appears that there is more to this story. Let us put the cards on the table so we can put this issue to rest."
- "I have a sense that there is really more to this story than what you have told me. Is there anything else that you would like to add?"

FISHING FOR EVIDENCE

When asked how he would respond to nonverbal signs of deceit during a job interview, Dr. Ekman offered this advice: "I would ask a number of follow-up questions and try to see how the applicant would handle them." His research suggests that the chance of uncovering deceit is directly related to our ability to ask good questions. Like a fishing net, good follow-up questions often can bring valuable information to the surface.

For example, if the candidate came up with a convoluted answer to your question about why he left the previous company, you might follow up with, "How much notice did you give your previous employer? Did your decision have anything to do with any personal disagreements? Were there any personality clashes?"

While the candidate answers your questions, compare what is said in words to how the body expresses emotions. Lie catchers listen with their eyes and ears for subtle clues like:

- Does the tone of voice go up at the end of a sentence?
- Does the applicant's voice hesitate?
- Do you notice small shrugs?
- When the person talks about a positive situation, are the eyebrows relaxed or drawn together?
- Do self-touching gestures increase while answering your question?
- Does the applicant assume a stiffer posture?
- Does the candidate become more quiet and withdrawn?

When you notice contradictions, don't just trust what the person is saying even though his words may be very convincing. Dr. Ekman cautions against premature judgments: "We can't find conclusive proof that the person has lied just by observing behavioral clues; all we can learn from them is that we had better do some more checking before taking the next step."

PROBING FOR MOTIVES BEHIND THE LIES

To uncover lies another way, search for the possible reasons, motives, and justifications for lying. One of the most common reasons why people lie is because they have developed a strong sense of loyalty to other people that outweighs their commitment to telling the truth.

Dr. Ekman offered two typical examples: "Let's say one of your children comes home past curfew and tells the younger sibling, 'Don't tell Mom or Dad!' The younger child has to decide whether to be loyal to the older sibling or to the parent. Or, what if a good friend asks you to meet his new girlfriend. He tells you, 'I want you to meet my new girlfriend. I am completely in love with her. She is the person I have been searching for all my life. I know she is right for me.' When you meet her, you find that she has nearly the same personality traits as his former wife. You know that your friend has had a long history of marital conflicts. When he asks you, 'Isn't she wonderful?' What do you say? Do you tell him what you really think to save your friend from a potential disappointment, or do you support his illusion by concealing the truth?"

Dr. Ekman has isolated 10 major patterns that people use to conceal the truth or falsify information. (See "The Classic Lies Customers Will Use on You.") While it's easy to recognize the motives after the lie has been exposed (like the fear of punishment in former President Nixon's case that was marked by his famous words "I am not a crook"), it takes a trained eye, solid skills, a great deal of patience, and experience to spot the signals, find the motive, search for the evidence, and uncover the truth.

UNDERSTANDING WHY PROSPECTS LIE

Salespeople often get angry or frustrated when they realize that their prospects have been lying to them. Dr. Ekman explains that prospects often get embarrassed by the fact that they really can't afford the product. When prospects say "I'll be back" or "I will think this over," the prime motive is often the fear that they won't be able to deal with a stressful situation. Says Dr. Ekman, "I recently looked at a piece of equipment, and when I asked for the price, it was so far beyond my budget that I told the salesman that I had to take some measurements first to see if it fit. I used this excuse to get out of the situation and avoid embarrassment."

When asked how he would have handled the situation if the roles had been reversed, Dr. Ekman answered, "I would say to the customer, 'I understand that this seems like a lot more money than what you thought about spending on this, but the product has so many more features, it lasts much longer, and it will retain its value much longer. In addition, there is a payment plan that really makes this affordable for almost everyone." Dr. Ekman suggests that salespeople should anticipate the client's fears and be prepared to deal with them in a polite and diplomatic fashion. Experienced salespeople learn how to reassure buyers and help them overcome their reluctance to talk about financial concerns.

BUILD TRUST—DON'T LET DECEPTION BEGET DECEPTION

While it is often frustrating to be deceived by a customer, sales people should resist the temptation to respond in kind.

Sales managers must educate salespeople that lying is not an option in the pursuit of a sale—even though their customers aren't always truthful. Dr. Ekman warns that there is a substantial difference between concealing your true feelings about your customers and concealing the truth about the qualities of your product. He cautions, "For example, if a salesperson says that a product is new when it is in fact used, the salesperson's lie may break the law and there may be serious consequences for the company and the salesperson."

Dr. Ekman believes that we are responsible for creating the conditions that favor the truth. For example, when people suspend their need for gaining an immediate advantage or hold back their desire for quick, short-term profits, mutual trust has a better chance of growing.

He cites an example from his own experience: "I like classical music, and I like to buy from one store in town that isn't known for low prices, but for quality service. For example, their salespeople can tell you the different versions of a symphony and they know the subtle details about the different recordings. To me, expert knowledge builds confidence, and I am willing to pay more money when I can get good advice."

CAVEAT FOR THE SELLER

In 1513, Machiavelli wrote in *The Prince:* "Men are so simple and yield so readily to the wants of the moment that he who will trick will always find another who will suffer himself to be tricked." Dr. Ekman says that often when people fall in love with a particular house, a certain car, or a special kind of high-tech equipment, "They stop acting rationally and become so preoccupied with the object that they cease to be sensitive to deceit."

While infatuation is often an invitation to exploitation, some buyers get hurt by their own self-deceptions and their lack of inside knowledge.

"Many times, customers are not as experienced as the salesperson," explains Dr. Ekman. "For example, in my lifetime I have purchased about seven cars. This puts me at a great disadvantage when I talk to a salesperson who may sell seven cars in a week. Salespeople are more experienced in being convincing, and most buyers can't tell if the salesperson is truthful to them."

In addition, Dr. Ekman believes that many salespeople are natural performers and most buyers don't notice the giveaway clues that betray the seller.

While we're all eager to protect ourselves against lies, we're most hurt when we're lied to or when other people in our profession practice deceit. While buyers are told caveat emptor ("Let the buyer beware") before every important purchase, in every selling situation the seller's moral judgment is challenged by four temptations:

- It is easier to fool unsuspecting people than to serve people.
- It takes less courage to hide the truth than to admit it.
- It takes less time to lie than it takes to build trust.
- It is easier to conceal the truth than to uncover deception.

On every call, salespeople have a choice to do what's right or what is easy and expedient. To do what's right is a question of moral judgment.

In 1785, Thomas Jefferson wrote a letter to Peter Carr sharing his thoughts on the subject: "Whenever you are to do a thing, though it can never be known but to yourself, ask yourself how you would act were all the world looking at you, and act accordingly." An old salesman I once knew put it in fewer words, "Always buy the truth, and never sell it."

ACTION STEPS

LIES & DECEPTION

1. When you are presenting to a customer and you see the muscles around the eyes deepen, go for a trial close.
2. Do not confront potential liars. Try to build bridges instead of widening gulfs.
3. Compare words to body language. Even when a person sounds convincing, if the body language betrays the person, be suspicious.
4. When you suspect people of being dishonest with you, ask probing questions to see how they handle the pressure.
5. In general, watch out for contradictions between what people tell you now and what they have said before, as well as between their verbal and nonverbal messages.
6. No matter the clues they give off, never assume that someone is lying. Just file away your suspicions and try to get at the truth later.

Chapter 14

Listening Power: Your Secret Weapon

Objective:

To explain specific methods you can put to use today to make you a more effective listener, and consequently a better salesperson.

Synopsis:

1. Selling is an exercise in discovering and satisfying customer needs. Without good listening capabilities, a salesperson cannot uncover a customer's needs.

2. We spend, on average, 50 percent of our time listening. Obviously, any activity that requires so much of our time must be important.

3. Without being able to listen to what people say, it is impossible to build effective relationships.

4. Salespeople usually listen poorly because:

   a) They are never shown how important it is to really listen to customers.

   b) They think that selling means persuading through talking.

   c) They assume they already know what the customer is going to say.

   d) They do not understand that customers do not know the trade lingo that they casually toss around in a conversation.

5. Good listening skills only work in conjunction with other effective sales techniques and prerequisites.

r. Lyman Steil tells his audience of high-level executives a story of three elderly English gentlemen riding on a train, sitting comfortably in the dining car. The first broke the silence, looking out the window and asking, "Is this Wembley?" The second glanced at his watch and replied, "No, it's Thursday." After a brief moment, the third nodded, "So am I. Let's have a Scotch and soda."

The audience chuckles, but Dr. Steil, a listening expert who has researched the field for dozens of years, gets quickly to the point. "On the average, we listen only at a 25 percent level of efficiency."

His techniques and concepts have received international attention since he helped develop a highly publicized listening skills training program for the Sperry Corporation.

Dr. Steil, professor at the University of Minnesota, founder and past president of the International Listening Association, uses innumerable ways to help his audience understand, accept, and apply his innovative concepts, like his famous Steil's LAW of listening. He writes on a blackboard: $L = A + W$, meaning listening equals ability plus willingness. If we don't have the ability, we can't communicate. "Not everybody's hard of hearing like these English gentlemen," he adds, "but practically speaking, executives who are unwilling to listen don't get any better results."

This chapter is an exclusive interview with Dr. Steil, who shares how his listening techniques could lead to increased sales success.

Dr. Steil, you've been in the business of selling hundreds of thousands of people on increasing their listening skills. Could you give us three major benefits of better listening skills that would apply to any sales executive?

Dr. Steil: There are many benefits. First, if you look at a workable definition of selling, you see that selling consists basically of

THE S-I-E-R FORMULA

In his lectures around the globe, Dr. Steil, known as Dr. Ear-Q, offers his S.I.E.R. Formula to help individuals understand their responsibility for active listening.

"Listening," he says, "is a four-part process." He calls the first part **Sensing**. Here, the listener needs to pay attention to the verbal and nonverbal expressions communicated by the sender. It is important to use all five senses for receiving the total message.

In the second part, described as **Interpreting**, we become responsible for assigning a comparable meaning to the messages received. "The effective listener remembers," warns Dr. Steil, "that words have no meaning—people have meaning." If you are not sure, ask questions to check if your interpretations are correct.

The third part, entitled **Evaluating**, is designed to weigh the information and to decide how to use it, "The best listeners," explains Dr. Steil, "delay judgment until their comprehension is complete and they have developed their skills in making judgments."

The last part, **Responding**, completes the active listening cycle. "If you apply the S.I.E.R. Formula in selling," promises Dr. Steil, "you'll be able to build better relationships and increase your income over the long run."

To many, listening is only a two-step process—hearing and responding. If you add two more skills, such as interpreting and evaluating, you should be able to increase your present listening power by 50 percent.

(1) identifying buyers' needs, and/or (2) creating buyers' needs, and (3) fulfilling buyers' needs. You can't identify or create needs or obviously fulfill needs without listening effectively and efficiently.

Second, listening is central to successful communication. Studies show that we spend, on the average, nearly 50 percent of our time in the process of listening. Most of us do not listen as well as we could or should. We have not been trained to do it in a focused and effective way.

Third, one might argue that human relationships are at the heart of productive, effective selling. We basically sell best and are sold best by people we feel related to. Listening proves to be the number one skill to create and improve human relationships. Listening is at the heart of selling, and the major benefit is heightened success.

> *In some of your articles you mentioned that most people*
> *make more than one major listening mistake every day.*
> *Could you give us some examples that relate to the world*
> *of selling?*

Examples abound, but let me tell you about a near miss. A sales manager recently told me about one of his salesmen who said, "Come with me on this call. I'm about to close a sale on a very large piece of machinery." The sale exceeded $750,000. The salesman had been working for a long period of time; he had done all of his needs assessment and created a good relationship. So, he worked up his final closing arguments. The sales manager agreed that he would just sit quietly by.

After a little bit of small talk, the salesman began, "You know, Sam, I've worked hard to bring us to this point, and I want to wrap it up. I have tried to isolate all the reasons why this is a good deal for you." And he launched into a fine closing presentation. After a few moments, the fellow across the desk, who obviously didn't have the time to listen to all of this said, "I'm already convinced. Just show me what I have to sign. I have some other things I have to do." The salesman, captured by his own voice, didn't hear any of that. He was too busy talking and telling Sam why this machine was a fantastic investment and that they ought to close, and so he continued.

After the buyer had interrupted the salesman three or four times and said, "Where do I sign?" and "I have other things to do," the salesman got irritated and said, "Look, I've only got 11 more minutes and I'll be finished with you." Now at that point the sales manager jumped in and said, "He has a fantastic sense of humor, doesn't he?" and said, "You sign right here." This man could literally have lost a $750,000 sale.

How do you explain this listening problem?
In this example, the salesman assumed that selling is basically a job of persuading through talking. As a consequence, he does not clearly, carefully, and patiently listen to the customer.

What other listening problems do you see in selling?
Many salespeople are too preoccupied with the short-term goal of getting the order, rather than working toward the long-term goal of being of service to a growing number of clients. For instance, the other day I had a meeting with the chairman of the board of a large bank. He emphasized the fact that many bankers have problems with applying good listening skills. He made the point that there are a lot of bank executives who listen very carefully to people who are coming in for the $100,000 loans, but they don't devote too much time to the person who comes in for the $1,000 loan. His point was fascinating because he said that the executive who is a long-term thinker will look at every person who comes in as a potential $100,000 piece of business. He said, "The $1,000 clients grow, and if they are receiving the $100,000 service each time they come in, we'll have part of their growing business for many years to come."

What are the major obstacles and barriers that prevent us from listening?
The most important obstacle is that most people never think about the importance of listening and consequently don't work at

TIPS	**4 TIPS ON LISTENING**

1 Before you answer a phone call, collect your mental energies so you will be ready to give your full attention to your caller. Don't be eating, reading, or talking to someone else.

2 Always answer the phone with your opposite hand and keep a pen in your writing hand to take down any important notes or information.

3 Often, what may seem to be a tedious exercise in putting up with an overly talkative purchasing agent can result in a salesperson gaining valuable insight into how a prospect's company operates.

4 Don't ignore your buyers, even if what they're saying doesn't seem important.

improving their skills and abilities. Our school system neglects this subject consistently.

A second barrier is that many salespeople think that selling is primarily a job of persuasion, and persuasion means talking. The typical poor sales rep is one who is eager to deliver a canned sales pitch. Many times he is insensitive to what the customer wants to hear and therefore antagonizes the prospect.

The third barrier is that many salespeople are having problems with not hearing fully what their customers have to say. They assume they know what someone is going to say before they say it, and quickly respond to it. What's worse, many even respond inappropriately while the customer is still talking.

The fourth barrier is the problem of understanding. There is quite often a significant vocabulary difference between buyer and

seller. That is particularly the case with salespeople who are techni-
cally very knowledgeable. Many times they meet buyers who are
not as knowledgeable, and they use a language that is crystal clear
to them, but their words have no meaning to the prospect. Edgar
Dale, a communications expert, coined a term for that called the
C.O.I.K. fallacy, which stands for "Clear, only if known."

*Why do most people assume that listening is a passive
activity?*

That assumption grows out of the fact most people haven't system-
atically thought about listening. One of the favorite questions that
we ask in our seminars is, "Who is primarily responsible for the success of the communication—the sender or the receiver?" What we
find is that 70 percent of the respondents say the sender. In our
society, we perceive sending as an active process, and we basically
look at receiving as a passive process. Only 20 to 25 percent say that
the receiver has the predominant responsibility. And [this fallacy]
leads to passive (and ineffective) listening.

*Is there a relationship that you have been able to identify
between the ability to listen to your own thoughts and the
ability to listen to other people?*

In a general sense, yes. People who are skilled in communicating well
with others are good communicators with self first. Many people
don't focus on the constant stream of thoughts that flow through
their minds or don't consider those messages to be important. If you
listen well to yourself, you position yourself to listen well to others.

How can you improve your listening skills?

Let me begin to answer this with a question. Imagine what
would happen if both salespeople and customers would agree to
minimally take 51 percent responsibility for listening.

You see, in selling we need to overcome the habit of blaming
either the salesperson or the customer for the breakdown of communication. The word *communication* comes from the Latin word

TELEPHONE LISTENING TECHNIQUES

In his extensive research, Dr. Steil found that most salespeople have not developed a systematic approach to telephone selling. "A lot of salespeople get into poor listening habits very quickly," he explains. "They think because a prospect answers the phone, he's ready to listen to their spiel."

Dr. Steil suggests asking questions like: "Do you have time? Can you listen for three minutes?" or "Do you have paper and pencil ready? I'd like to share some important things with you."

He advises allowing time for the listener to shift gears. More important: Create a brief concentration phase to collect your mental energies before you make or answer a call.

Have you ever thought about exactly where to put your telephone? If you're right-handed, place your telephone on the left side of your desk for three reasons:

You won't have the cord dangling over your workspace, you will have your right hand free to take notes, and you don't waste time shifting the telephone to the other hand.

When do you answer your telephone? Dr. Steil warns: "Don't answer your telephone in a compulsive fashion. First, stop your conversation, clear your mind, and shift gears away from what you were doing. Have a pad of paper and pencil ready. Once you are ready, no matter what ring it is, answer the telephone with your opposite-handed side."

> Dr. Steil feels that this approach allows you to listen more effectively right from the very first second. He suggests that during the first 15 seconds callers tell you who they are, where they are from, what company they are with, and why they are calling. Many sales executives don't hear that information, because they are still working on a project, shifting hands, or busy searching for something to write on.

communis, which means to achieve commonality between sender and receiver. If we want to achieve this commonality, we need to take no less than 51 percent responsibility for active listening. We also need to stop believing that sales success is limited to a successful close. If there has been good communication and the buyer chooses not to buy, it does not mean that the salesperson has failed. Even though you have not been able to put the bacon and eggs on the table that day, your good listening skills may put a steak on your table in the long run. The successful sales professional is one who knows that we have to prepare for the future today.

Do you have any evidence that suggests that good listening skills can improve long-term sales success?

There are two independent surveys that may give you some idea on how important listening can be for the bottom line. First, a large retail organization found that 68 percent of the customers who stopped buying from them indicated that they did so because the store's salespeople were indifferent to their needs.

Second, about six years ago, we were working with a company and tried to identify their customers' primary reasons for buying. They put service on the top of the list of five major reasons. When we asked the customers what service meant to them, they said, "They listen and help us fulfill our needs."

What are the major listening techniques that a salesperson should use in every call?

First, you need to develop a positive attitude toward listening. You may tell yourself: "I need to care; I need to be concerned; I need to take and make the time; I need to truly be other-oriented; I need to listen to you from your perspective, from where you're coming; I need to build a relationship."

Second, the effective listener needs to recognize that when customers have problems on their minds, they will not listen well to information or persuasion. They won't be sold until those problems or concerns are dealt with.

Some salespeople can hear at a rate of 400–500 words per minute. How do you harness your excess mental energy when you face a person who speaks at a rate of 160 words per minute?

The average rate of speed of speech is somewhere between 125 and 180 wpm. When a speaker speaks more slowly, we need to adjust to that speed. The poor listener usually wastes the advantage by going off on mental tangents, solving other problems, wanting to shut the guy up so they can talk, and so forth. The effective listener harnesses some of that advantage; he uses it.

How can you do that?

There is a four-step technique that is easy to remember by thinking of the word EARS. E stands for evaluate; A stands for anticipate; R stands for review; and S stands for summarize. That's one way to keep you tuned to what the prospect is saying.

Using the EARS technique seems logical, but it doesn't sound like something related to fun or immediate gain. How can salespeople avoid slipping into daydreams when they're listening to a boring prospect?

One of the things we know about poor listeners is that they are very quick to call something uninteresting, dull, not important, et cetera. The good listeners that we find are of a different bent;

they are selfish, but in a very positive way. They're looking for the value of listening. They're constantly saying to themselves, "How can I use this; where will it work; how can I help someone else; how will this pay off?"

One of the great dilemmas of listening is that we simply will never know the value of listening until after we're down the road, after we've listened, after we've responded, after somebody calls us on it. A lot of times we listen to boring people, and when they're done, we say to ourselves, "Boy, this was a waste of time. That guy didn't have anything to say; he didn't say it well." But consider that if you want an ounce of gold, you throw away some 250 tons of rubble. If you want a bushel of wheat, you throw away the chaff. If you want fine jewels, you throw away the waste. My point is that for any value item, there is work and there is waste. Unfortunately, we have a tendency in this society with our fast-paced approach to life to look for immediate satisfaction, immediate gratification. Short term, as opposed to long term. What we quite often expect of the speaker is to put all the gold, all the jewels, all the wheat, all the valuable things right up front. I thought about this very carefully. I don't know many speakers, customers, clients, friends, mates, children, who put all the gold right up front. In this interview today, we might have intermingled an ounce of gold among all the rubble.

> *Does good listening include the interpretation of*
> *a prospect's body language?*

When someone is communicating an idea, a thought, a feeling, et cetera, they do so with more than just words. There have been tremendous gains in the last 20 years in the area of nonverbal communication. At the same time, I am very cautious. There are a lot of books on the market that suggest that certain nonverbal messages automatically mean certain things.

You can't say that crossed arms always means that the buyer is defensive. One never knows what's really going on in the buyer's mind, unless you ask focused questions that can clarify your impressions. You could use a probing question and ask, "How do you feel about that particular feature?" Or you could make a statement like, "I see you're a little hesitant about this." You need to use these techniques to test your assumptions.

> *Every salesperson has the responsibility to be understood as*
> *well as to understand. What are the techniques that one*
> *can use to get buyers and prospects to listen better?*

If you have something of interest, something of value and of significance to say, your chances that the buyer is willing to listen will increase. To ensure good listening, you need to be succinct, to the point, to present the information from the other person's point of view. If you organize your ideas in advance, you'll say it well, and it will be fun to listen to you. But if you don't care to prepare, you shouldn't be surprised when your prospects don't care to listen to you.

> *How easy is it to become a better listener?*

It's not easy at all. We're talking about an extraordinarily complex process. We're talking on one hand about a knowledge factor; we're secondly talking about an attitudinal, motivational factor; and, third, we're talking about a behavior or skills factor. And the reality is that you, I, and all others listen the way we listen because we learned to listen that way. We haven't been trained to do it well; we don't do it well; and to think that there is what we call a "quick fix" is totally absurd. It takes focus; it takes energy, commitment, and practice, practice, practice. But the best news of all is that everyone can be better—and profit!

ACTION STEPS

LISTENING SKILLS

1. Remember that it is your responsibility to understand what the customer tells you.
2. Make good communication your goal. If you close the sale, great. If not, you have at least begun to build a foundation for the future.
3. Do whatever you have to ahead of time so that you are prepared to listen whenever you walk into a customer's office.
4. To stay focused on an individual, use the EARS (Evaluate, Anticipate, Review, Summarize) technique.

Chapter 15

Neuro-Linguistic Sales Programming: The Unfair Advantage

Objective:

To explain the revolutionary techniques of neuro-linguistic programming that will help you monitor eye movements to accurately reveal your customers' thought patterns.

Synopsis:

1. Human eye movements provide clues to what your customers may be thinking about.
2. NLP techniques can help you determine how to adjust your approach to individual customers.
3. When your customers look:
   - Up and to the left, they are remembering a visual image from the past. This is a visual person.
   - Up and to the right, they are creating a visual image they have not seen before. This person is a dreamer.
   - Down and to the left, they are remembering words or sounds from the past. This is an auditory person.

Irma has her fortune read every year, and she is amazed at how much fortune tellers know about her. Yet Irma is no dummy. Instead of visiting one, she consults three or four in different parts of the city. Invariably the tea leaf reader, the palm reader, and the astrologer give her readings that are so similar as to leave her breathless. At the last go-around they told her she was going to get married in March. How is that for coincidence among soothsayers who don't even know one another?

Coincidence? Well, not exactly. These fortune tellers are really "cold readers," sophisticated mind readers who convince clients whom they have never met that they know everything about their personalities and problems. In that respect they share a most valuable asset with the peak performers of the sales world, those men and women who have developed their sensitive skills to sonar precision. You, the serious sales professional, now have a tool at your mental fingertips that enables you to deliberately develop your own intuitive awareness and to program your customers to give you the expected buying response. You may not want to be a cold reader, but you can become a master communicator.

NEURO-LINGUISTIC SALES PROGRAMMING

Neuro-Linguistic Sales Programming (NLSP) provides new dimensions in observing people and communicating with them. It is the science of face-to-face communication and explains how professional communicators use words and gestures to program the minds of other people, dramatically opening up a whole new world of sales development and sales success.

Neuro-Linguistic Programming (NLP) was developed by John Grinder, a professor of linguistics, and Richard Bandler, a

Expert Advice: This chapter features contributions from Dr. Donald J. Moine and John H. Herd, coauthors of *Modern Persuasion Strategies: The Hidden Advantage in Selling.* A well-regarded sales psychologist, Moine is also the author of *Ultimate Selling Power* (www.salesandmarketingbootcamp.com).

therapist/physicist, at the University of California. By combining the most effective strategies of Gestalt psychology, systems theory, cybernetics, psycholinguistics, and persuasion patterns, Bandler and Grinder laid the groundwork for the emerging science of NLP.

HOW TO READ YOUR CUSTOMER'S THOUGHTS

Did you know, for example, that human eye movements accurately reveal thought patterns? This remarkable finding comes directly from modern neuropsychology and is of great importance to the sales professional.

Ask a friend, "Have you seen a good movie lately?" and watch her look up and to the left as she says, "Let's see . . ." before she can give you an answer. What did she do? She searched her memory bank and literally saw again a face or a scene from the movie. Her eye movements up and left were the giveaway. Had she looked down and to the right, it would have revealed something different about her thought patterns and values.

The eyes are connected to parts of the cerebral cortex, where memories are stored. Eye movements are not random. As you talk with a person in casual conversation or on a sales call, his or her eye movements reveal the type of information he or she is pulling from his or her memory banks. This is your clue for how to sell him or her.

EYE MOVEMENTS

Here is what eye movements tell about your listener. When he is looking up and left, he is remembering something seen in the past. This is called an eidetic or remembered visual image.

When you listen carefully to his speech, he is likely to use visual words and phrases such as, "That's not clear to me," "Can you shed a little more light on that subject?" or, "Hey, that's a bright idea." Even his language reveals he's thinking visually.

How do you sell effectively to that customer? You paint word pictures, using visual words, because you are now talking the customer's language. A basic finding from psychology is that we trust people who are like us. To sell effectively to this customer, you should communicate: "I am like you. We talk the same language. We understand each other—you can trust me."

What if your customer looked up and right? She is using her imagination to create something she has not seen before: a dream house, or a car she wants to win . . . or she may be making up a fib.

To effectively sell this person, paint word pictures about the future: how beautiful something will be, as in "Can you imagine the expression on your neighbor's face when you drive up in this new Cadillac?" Top producers do this intuitively.

What if your customer is looking down and left? This person is accessing information stored in the auditory parts of his cerebral cortex. In a manner of speaking, she is talking to herself or is repeating something her husband or business associate might have said.

AUDITORY

Listen to the words your customer uses: "Hey, that rings a bell," "We're not in harmony on that point," or "That really struck a chord with me."

There are hundreds of examples of visual and auditory ways of speaking. Listen for them and then speak your customer's language. This is what top salespeople do. And when you do it, you cannot help but be more successful. To sell the sound-oriented customer, use sound-based words and phrases. Include testimonials. They are the positive words that other customers say about you and your product. This may not sell the visual person, but it is effective with the auditory customer.

KINESTHETIC

What if your customer keeps looking down and right? What kind of information is he accessing from his memory banks?

This type of customer monitors his feelings. Even highly intelligent customers check out their hunches and gut-level reactions. Don't look down on this type of customer. He is capable of making excellent decisions. To sell him, speak his language. "Does that feel OK to you?" "Are we in step?" "Can you grasp the impact of that?"

What are the dynamics behind this? We trust people whom we perceive to be like us. *The Harvard Business Review* reports that the first person hired is the one most like the boss and the first person fired is the least like him. It may not be fair, but that is the way of the world. The only question now is, "How can I communicate to the customer that I am like him and that he can trust me?" NLSP offers the answers.

OTHER ANSWERS OFFERED BY NLSP

In addition to reading eye movements and listening for sensory language, NLSP tells us exactly how to sell to different people. The human mind resembles a sophisticated biocomputer. Once you know how a person has been programmed, you can speak "human computer" language and sell that person. The only way the person can resist you is to resist him- or herself. For most of us that isn't natural.

NLSP has much to say about our decision-making strategies, including how customers make purchase decisions. Most people go through several steps before making a choice. Each of these steps is like the digit of a phone number. An average producer may know all the digits, yet fail to get them in correct order. The top producer, by contrast, not only discovers your exact purchasing strategy but plays it back in its right sequence. Naturally you buy from the person who can reach you and fill your needs best.

You can begin now by simply replaying your customer's thought processes in their precise order. You will begin to close more sales. The fine points can come later.

NEURO-LINGUISTIC SALES TRAINING

NLSP is highly entertaining and inspiring to salespeople, especially when presented live at a training session or at conventions. It lends itself easily to demonstrations and dramatic role plays. Once salespeople in an audience see it in action, they are sold on its utility and ability to make them more money. Select your trainer carefully. Make sure that in addition to a thorough NLP background, he or she has a success pattern in personal selling.

ACTION STEPS

NEURO-LINGUISTIC PROGRAMMING

1. To sell to the visual customer, use words that conjure up visual images he or she can imagine.
2. To sell to the dreamer, paint pictures of the future, such as what he or she will look like driving a new car or in a new house.
3. To sell to the auditory customer, use sound-based words and phrases as well as testimonials.
4. To sell to the sensitive customer, try to let the customer know that his or her feelings are important to you and that you both need to feel good about any decision.

Chapter 16

Procrastinating Clients: How Do You Handle Procrastinators?

Objective:

To provide you with clear-cut advice for dealing with procrastinating customers and help you speed up the sales cycle.

Synopsis:

1. To handle procrastinating prospects, salespeople must both manage their own negative thoughts and uncover the sources of the prospects' reasons for procrastinating.

2. Perfectionism and sensitivity to coercion are among the many reasons why prospects put off the buying decision.

"Procrastinating clients don't need to drive you crazy," asserts Dr. David Burns, Philadelphia psychiatrist and author of the best seller *Feeling Good*. Think about how you've handled your last procrastinating prospect. Remember the familiar phrases: "I've got to think about it," or "I'll get back to you," or "I'll talk to my boss (my lawyer, my accountant, my friend, et cetera) about it." If you are in a depressed market segment, you may have listened to putoffs like "It's not the right time; everything is slow; it's a darn good idea, but we have to wait."

"The first step," explains Dr. Burns, "is to pinpoint why the client procrastinates." That's not an easy task, since it requires a great deal of tact, sensitivity, and empathy. "Don't get judgmental, but try to see the problem through the client's eyes," says Dr. Burns. "Your own attitude toward the client who procrastinates is very crucial. Don't get demanding, coercive, defensive, or hostile. These are some of the most common behavioral traps salespeople need to avoid."

In his book, Dr. Burns explains 12 different types of mind-sets most commonly associated with procrastination and indecisiveness. Reading about them can give you greater understanding and sensitivity toward people who seem to resist you. This can be the first step toward better rapport and, ultimately, a sale.

HOW DO YOU HANDLE PROCRASTINATORS?

One common trap to look out for is perfectionism. The client isn't totally certain he should buy your product. He thinks he should always be right and is possibly afraid of making a mistake.

Another trap is sensitivity to coercion—the client may sense your eagerness and feel pushed. She then decides she has to resist you to stay in control.

These are just two of numerous reasons why a client might be slow in closing a deal, while from your point of view there seems to be no rational basis for any reluctance.

VERBAL TECHNIQUES

"Your best approach," advises Dr. Burns, summarizing his clinical experiences with countless procrastinators, "is to employ simple verbal techniques such as (1) Empathy, (2) Inquiry, and/or (3) Multiple Choice."

If your client responds to your closing question with, "I've got to think about it," you could easily follow up with an inquiry like, "What are some of the issues you have to think about?" Or you may directly focus on the client's resistance by asking, "What are some of the things that are holding you back? Would you share some of them with me?"

Be sure to communicate positive attitudes. If your nonverbal expressions signal defensive attitudes, you could easily reinforce the client's (irrational) defenses.

Imagine this reply to your enthusiastic sales pitch: "I've got to talk to my boss about this purchase." If you are unprepared, this surprising answer may take the wind out of your sails and leave you speechless. But with a little advance preparation and role playing, you may disarm the procrastinator quickly with, "Of course you do. What are some of the things you would talk to him (or her) about?"

This allows you to agree with the reluctant prospect. This approach puts you both on the same team and encourages the prospect to open up and trust you. By responding with empathy ("Of course you do"), you put yourself in the client's position; by using a judgmental or defensive reply like, "Why can't you decide on this as you promised . . . ," you'd be reinforcing the client's hesitancy, and he or she may even add you to the list of subjects to be discussed with his or her boss.

"In some cases, the client won't respond to your empathy and/or inquiry technique," adds Dr. Burns. "That should not hold you back from using multiple-choice questions."

Let's say the buyer in the example above mumbles a reply like, "Oh, I've got to get his opinion on this purchase." You may follow up with, "Would you be exploring if this is a good purchase in connection with a competitor's product, or would you be wondering about the financing?"

"Display an attitude of genuine caring. Paraphrase your questions in a noncoercive yet open way," counsels Dr. Burns. The key is to balance empathy with firmness.

SELF-MANAGEMENT

"Asking questions and displaying positive attitudes is only half the battle," explains Dr. Burns. "Dealing with procrastinators also calls for managing your own negative thoughts and feelings."

Most salespeople tend to overlook the relationship between thoughts and feelings. Dr. Burns writes in *Feeling Good*: "The most important thing to realize is that all your moods are created by your thoughts, not by how other people are treating you." In other words, the things you are telling yourself silently about your client can influence your moods negatively, and the moment you let yourself feel irritable or frustrated, you can kiss the sale goodbye.

For example, as you hear the client stall, you may say to yourself, "I have an excellent product. He shouldn't do this. I've offered the best possible price. He's got no right to be so unreasonable." Or you might get mentally self-critical like: "Gee, I really should be able to close this deal. What's wrong with me?"

"Your emotions follow your thoughts just as surely as baby ducks follow their mother," writes Dr. Burns. "But the fact that the baby ducks follow faithfully along doesn't prove that the mother knows where she's going."

PREPARATION

"You can prepare yourself before you see potential procrastinators," he explains. "Remember not to defend your self-esteem by putting the other person down. In the last analysis, only one person can make you happy or miserable, and that person is you. And if you're thinking about yourself in a positive and realistic way, you feel good and have the world's most potent sales force at your disposal—self-esteem."

Don't read motives into the customer by telling yourself, "He enjoys being resistant. He just wants to give me a hard time." This prevents you from uncovering the real reasons underlying his procrastination. Remember that handling procrastination has nothing to do with getting the other person to give in to you; the solution to resolving the client's hesitancy lies in allowing it to be expressed. Showing genuine concern for your client as a human being—and not as an object to be manipulated—is as crucial to an effective sales career as it is to a happy marriage or a lasting friendship.

GUIDELINES

Thus, the steps for handling the procrastinating client are:

1. Prepare yourself for a possible delaying maneuver—before the call.
2. Pinpoint the reasons and show your openness, your empathy, and your understanding (don't judge—observe).
3. Manage your self-talk. Don't put the client down; don't put yourself down.
4. Help the client realistically appraise her reasons for and against buying now. And if it's not in her best interest to buy your product now, urge her not to. She'll respect you, and you'll feel better about yourself and make out better in the long run.

"Selling to procrastinators can be very rewarding and profitable," concludes Dr. Burns. "It's like Zen. When you want the sale most, it moves beyond your reach. Instead, you temporarily abandon your preoccupation with control and success. As you open yourself to your client's experience, you are creating new space which is needed to dissolve the client's hesitancy. Once the pressure is removed, your client will be able to objectively reappraise your proposals (with your guidance) and make a decision.

"No matter what the outcome, you've created a win/win situation and you're ready to make your next call without the burden of unfinished business and most likely with the satisfaction of another sale."

ACTION STEPS

PROCRASTINATING CLIENTS

1. Prepare ahead of time for a potential procrastinator.
2. Pinpoint the reasons fueling procrastination.
3. Manage your self-talk so you're not putting yourself or the prospect down.
4. Be open and honest with the customer about whether this is a good time to buy or not. This will build the relationship.

PART III

UNDERSTANDING

YOURSELF

Chapter 17

Dealing with Anxiety: Get Control of Stress and Boost Your Sales

Objective:

To help you determine the seeds of your fears, phobias, and anxieties, and to give you specific methods for addressing these impediments to growth in business and your personal life.

Synopsis:

1. The best way to deal with anxieties is to confront them head-on.

2. To determine the cause of your anxieties or phobias, examine your intimate relationships, your career path, and your recent sales appointments.

3. If you have difficulty expressing emotions, are unsure about your career, or harbor long-suppressed emotional troubles, then you are a candidate for anxiety.

4. Fearful people are characterized by niceness, a keen imagination, lack of confidence, desire to please, conflict avoidance, desire to be perfect, and denial.

5. To rid yourself of anxiety, the anxiety itself must become part of the cure.

Anxiety, sometimes called the fear of impending disaster, is not a pleasant emotion, yet it tends to trouble people who are pleasant, kind, and outgoing. For example, Willard Scott, NBC's famous weatherman, experienced frightening panic attacks prior to live broadcasts. People who suffer from panic disorders often fear that they will lose control, go crazy, or have a heart attack and die. Although panic attacks usually disappear within a short time, they leave people feeling humiliated and convinced that there is something wrong with them.

Many salespeople secretly suffer from fears, phobias, and anxieties. They may fear discussing the subject openly. They're afraid of being called a "wimp," "chicken," or worse. Are you afraid of reading this article? If you are, you may be suffering from what Dr. David Burns calls "emotophobia"—the fear of negative emotions.

There are other forms of anxiety, such as hypochondriasis (the fear of getting sick), social anxiety (the fear of people), or such phobias as the fear of heights, the fear of flying, or the fear of riding in elevators. Many famous people have suffered from anxieties. Frederick the Great became anxious and nearly fainted when he had to put on a new coat. Frederic Chopin, the Polish composer, was afraid of the dark. In his 30s Sigmund Freud (the father of psychoanalysis) suffered from travel anxiety.

Many salespeople turn into nervous wrecks before calling on a new prospect or delivering an important presentation to a group of buyers. Many sales managers notice their hearts thumping faster during an unexpected report to the board of directors or before giving a speech.

How do you cope with the palpitations, dry mouth syndrome, sweaty palms, churning in your stomach, or strange feelings of weakness during those moments when you're expected to feel strong, confident, and secure? Anxiety is a puzzling psychological phenomenon, the most common mental health disorder in the United States. Anxiety can lead intelligent people to act like incompetent fools. It makes people miss appointments, say no to great opportunities, lose big sales, or even lose their jobs.

Many times feelings of anxiety are stimulating, healthy, and productive—some Navy pilots say that anxiety makes them more alert. At other times anxiety can be so strong that it leaves people trembling with fear.

Anxiety tends to isolate people. Some anxiety sufferers are too embarrassed or scared to share their feelings with anyone. Why? At the heart of anxiety lie shame and denial. Anxiety-prone people often deny such feelings as anger or frustration; at other times they may suppress a burning desire. Psychological research shows that suppressed emotions are sometimes stored without consequences, but at other times they are transformed into a wide range of puzzling physical symptoms of anxiety.

HOW DO ANXIOUS PEOPLE COPE?

When feelings of anxiety begin to trouble you, what do you do? Here are the three most common ways people cope with anxiety:

Avoidance or denial. Many people who suffer from the symptoms of anxiety won't admit their anxious thoughts or feelings. They refuse to acknowledge their fears even to people close to them, and suffer secretly, fearing that there is something seriously wrong with them. They are very careful to avoid feared situations or even thoughts that could produce anxiety. Avoidance of anxiety only makes the problem worse and tends to limit personal and professional growth.

Seeking comfort. Many anxious people seek out experiences that promise a change in their mood, such as watching TV, drinking alcohol, or taking drugs. While reduced stress may lessen the physical symptoms of anxiety, the cause of anxiety survives temporary mood transformations. When feelings of anxiety persist or increase, professional help is sought, and most physicians will be sympathetic and prescribe a mood stabilizing medication.

Seeking solutions. While taking mood stabilizing medications is only aimed at treating the symptoms of anxiety, there are a number of new and tested techniques and therapies that can help people understand the dynamic forces governing their feelings of anxiety and learn to leave their own greatest fears behind—forever.

THE FEELING GOOD HANDBOOK

Dr. David Burns, a leading psychiatrist at the Presbyterian Medical Center in Philadelphia, is clinical associate professor of psychiatry at the University of Pennsylvania School of Medicine and the author of two best-selling books. Dr. Burns suggests that anxiety can often be treated effectively without drugs. In fact, patients who follow his treatment are often symptom-free within a short period of time.

Dr. Burns has taught these techniques to his patients and fellow therapists with great success, and he has developed an easy-to-apply workbook called *The Feeling Good Handbook*.

In the following interview, Dr. Burns shares how he helps his patients conquer fears, phobias, and many different types of chronic anxieties. Unafraid of disclosing his own fears, he candidly tells how he overcame his fear of blood as a medical student, how he won over anxiety before lecturing at a symposium at Harvard, and how he kept anxiety from limiting his performance during important television interviews while promoting his first best-selling book, *Feeling Good*.

INTERVIEWING THE PSYCHIATRIST

What is your definition of anxiety?
Dr. Burns: It is a feeling of nervousness, worry, or fear. Anxiety has a definite future focus. People imagine that something bad is about to happen to them.

How is anxiety different from depression?
People who feel depressed have the sensation that the bad thing has already occurred, while people who feel anxious imagine that the bad thing is about to happen. For example, people who feel depressed may say to themselves, "Everyone knows that I am a loser." People who experience public speaking anxiety may tell themselves, "As soon as I open my mouth, everyone will know what a fool I am."

In that case people know why they feel anxious. What about situations where people feel anxious, but don't know why?

When most people get anxious, they can't identify what causes their feelings of distress. The medical profession calls this "free-floating" anxiety. Some doctors think it is a biological disorder, and many doctors prescribe drugs to alleviate the symptoms. However, I do not believe that anxiety is usually "free-floating." The cause can nearly always be traced, although this requires persistence.

SUPPRESSING ANGER OFTEN CREATES ANXIETIES

How can you pinpoint the real cause of anxiety?

In my opinion, when people are feeling anxious, they are usually disturbed about something that they are pushing out of their minds. Something that's really important to them is not acknowledged, but hidden and buried. When I ask these patients, they usually say that everything in their lives is fine, they are happy in their jobs, they are happy in their marriages, everything is great. Yet they are carrying some major problem inside that they don't like to admit to themselves—they are really unhappy about something that is causing their anxiety.

Can you give me an example?

Yes, I can give you a personal example. Not too long ago, I felt anxious for about four days. I had a hectic schedule and did not pay too much attention to the symptoms. Finally, I said to my wife, "I have been feeling anxious, but I haven't a clue as to why." She laughed and said, "Don't you remember that you have been talking to the department chairman about your promotion and you got real upset?" I immediately realized that I had pushed that out of my mind, and I became aware that it was still bothering me. So I got on the phone and called him, and we worked out the problem. After the call my anxiety disappeared instantly.

Did your suppressed emotions cause the anxiety?

Yes, I did not connect with my feelings right away. When people get upset, they react in many different ways. In my own case, I begin to get kind of sarcastic, or cold and distant, but there is part of me that says, "I am not upset." It's almost as if there were two halves of the brain that do not communicate very well with each other. One half communicates with people in a friendly and pleasant way, while the other half knows that you are really upset about something. It is common that people who have a pleasing personality don't always know when they get upset or angry. In fact, many salespeople suffer from holding back their anger or frustrations because they are expected to please their customers.

DON'T DENY NEGATIVE EMOTIONS, EXPRESS THEM

So free-floating anxiety disappears once these feelings are acknowledged and expressed?

Yes. We often find a connection between phobias and repressed anger. For example, one of my former patients, a very successful businessman, called me a few months ago and said, "Dr. Burns, my airplane phobia came back!" He asked to see me in an emergency session. I knew from a previous conversation that one of his business associates had an affair with his secretary, which caused an uproar in his office. I asked him, "Are you sure that everything is okay in your life?" He said, "Yes." I asked, "Are you mad at someone?" He said, "No." I kept probing and he kept denying. Finally, about 10 minutes before the end of the session, he said, "Dr. Burns, will you get off my back about this? We had a marvelous party at my home last night, and all the top executives came. People really had a ball. When I got up this morning to clean up, I found one of my associates sleeping on the couch with our new receptionist." I asked my patient, "Wasn't this the same guy you wanted to fire a year ago because he had an affair with your secretary?" He said, "Oh, I see what you mean. I should have given this guy a piece of my mind!" At the time he couldn't get angry, and that's why his phobia had returned.

> *Did his symptoms disappear after he became aware of his*
> *hidden feelings?*

Yes, the very moment he admitted how angry he felt, his anxiety disappeared. Knowing how and when to express your feelings is a very important skill that can enrich your life and make you a more complete and successful human being.

HOW SECRET DESIRES CAN CAUSE ANXIETY

> *I think that many salespeople can relate to what you are*
> *saying about holding back anger while you are trying to be*
> *nice. What are other causes of anxiety?*

It can be something that we strongly desire, but for some reason we feel that we have to deny this desire. Suppressed desire can make us feel anxious.

> *Can you give me an example?*

I treated a young M.B.A. graduate who worked in the marketing department of a large company. One day he was scheduled to fly to a sales convention with his boss. As he got ready for the trip, he developed an overwhelming fear of flying. He asked his wife to come with him to the airport, thinking that it would help overcome his fear, but the closer they got to the airport, the more his fear intensified. He felt bewildered because he had never had an airplane phobia in his life. They turned around and went back home. He called his boss and said, "You can fire me if you want, but there is no way I can get on that airplane to attend the convention."

When he came to see me, he felt embarrassed and assured me that everything in his life was fine. He told me that he liked his work and loved his wife, he was happy about their new baby, and he kept insisting that there was nothing that bothered him. After about six sessions of this denial he suddenly admitted that there might be important feelings that needed to be addressed. He explained that a neighbor who was about to retire was looking for someone to take over his business, which was quite lucrative. Since this neighbor had no children who could take over the business, he had offered extremely generous terms to my patient. He had worked part-time for this neighbor since high school and admired this man greatly. I asked him how he felt about that business proposition, and he admitted that he was very excited about the idea of having his own store and that he loved the prospect of being able to control his own future. His face lit up as he was describing his dream of owning his own business, but he felt that he was not allowed to think about it because he thought that his wife and his father might not approve of his taking a big risk. He also felt that his boss would think that he was disloyal to the company.

How did he solve this dilemma?
We developed ideas for talking over the problem with his wife and his boss. To his surprise, they both encouraged him. In fact, his boss told him that he would be always welcome to come back if things did not turn out, and his wife was happy that he had the desire to become more independent. He no longer felt trapped, the symptoms disappeared, and our therapy came to a successful and rapid conclusion.

ANXIETY IS OUR BODY'S APPEAL FOR AWARENESS

It seems that denying important feelings becomes the main cause of anxiety.
Exactly. Denial stands in the way of insight. I keep reminding my patients, "I really think that there is something in your life that's important to you that you are not telling me," and they keep insisting that they are holding nothing back. But somewhere

between the sixth and the tenth session they suddenly say, "Oh, by the way, I hate my job."

The examples you have shared seem to show that anxiety is somehow our body's appeal for awareness.
Yes, you are right. The body is screaming, "You better pay attention to your real feelings. If you keep denying your feelings, I will keep producing phobias." But most people go on unaware because they don't want to deal with conflict. We're afraid of conflict.

Why?
Because we think we have to please everybody. Or because we were raised to believe that we're not supposed to have negative feelings. Or because we assume that working toward a bold dream would mean betrayal to the people we love. So, you're right, anxiety is an appeal for awareness. The recovery from anxiety is particularly rewarding and joyous because people become more aware of who they are on the inside. They stop being so excessively preoccupied with how others see them, they know what's important to them, and they begin to grow to higher levels of awareness and responsibility.

THE CLUES THAT LEAD US TO THE CAUSES OF ANXIETY

How can we increase our awareness?
The first step would be to look at your marriage or your intimate relationships. I have developed a relationship satisfaction scale that I ask my patients to take every week.

The score tells you how happy your relationship is. The second area you want to look at is your career. Ask yourself: Is there anything about my work, my boss, or my customers that is bothering me? Third, just pull out your appointment book and think of the appointments you had. You may discover that you started worrying right after meeting with someone. This can sometimes help pinpoint the cause of your anxiety. Sometimes you may have to ask someone close to you to point out the elephant standing next to you that you haven't noticed.

What would be the next step?
It's not enough to just increase awareness; we also need to take the appropriate course of action. Awareness without action rarely leads to progress. The appropriate action is often as simple as to express your feelings to somebody. When people begin to open up in a meaningful way, it will often improve their lives and their relationships.

WHAT PEOPLE FEAR MOST IN THEIR CAREERS

You have seen many people with career conflicts. What causes people to feel anxious about their careers?
I used to see a number of first-year law students at the University of Pennsylvania Law School who were suffering from anxieties before exams. On the surface they appeared to be nothing more than temporary performance anxieties, but once I got to talk to these law students, I discovered a common thread in their complaints. They did not know why they were in law school.

Some were really smart but could not think of anything else to do. Others went there because their parents thought that they should be lawyers, but they did not find a lot of meaning in that choice. So, when they were suddenly faced with a high-pressure, demanding environment where they were placed in a group of highly competitive and smart people, they experienced intense levels of anxiety. They had never decided that they really wanted to be there and to succeed in that place. They were just there to please someone else.

Do you suggest that their inability to find meaning in pursuing a law career caused their anxieties?
Yes.

How did you help them?
For all of them, the solution would be the same. Once they became aware that they never made a real commitment to becoming a lawyer,

they realized the need for either leaving the school or making a conscious choice to stay. In reality, none of them ultimately chose to drop out, although nearly all of them had that thought when they first came to me. One student decided to become an entertainment lawyer who handles movie stars. Another decided that he would open a small general practice in the Midwest. Once they decided on a clear goal, they were able to make a deeper commitment to their work, and their anxiety disappeared. They could endure the stress of law school because they knew that their effort was personally meaningful.

That's interesting, because the most successful people I've ever interviewed seem to be very clear about their purpose in life.

Clarity of purpose is an important key to success.

ANXIOUS PEOPLE FEAR EMOTIONS

You said earlier that sometimes the most appropriate action anxious people can take is to express their feelings. What holds people back from doing that?

As I emphasized in *The Feeling Good Handbook,* many people are afraid of their feelings. They have difficulty accepting how they really feel inside. For example, I once treated a hard-working physician. He toiled 16 hours a day and had always been anxious and depressed. He told me that he had really never had a happy moment in the past 30 years. He was overly preoccupied with pleasing everybody and never thought about getting his own needs met. He had never learned how to express his own feelings, and although he said that he was happily married, his life was not filled with joy. One day he complained that he never felt close to his son, who studied medicine. He said that his conversations with his son were always very brief and superficial. So I suggested, "Sometimes when you are talking with your son, perhaps you could tell him that you love him, but that you find your conversations some what superficial. You might tell him that you sometimes feel lonely and would like to feel closer to him."

How did he respond to that?

He thought that I was an oddball, because normal people would not say things like that to their son. His reaction was typical. He came up with 25 reasons why he should never express his inner feelings to his son or to anyone else, for that matter. People who suffer from anxiety have a great fear of experiencing emotions. They follow the unwritten rule that says a human being must never feel upset. As soon as they begin to feel anxious, they get involved in a tremendous struggle to fight their inner feelings. What they fear most is becoming a real human being.

DON'T TRY TO CREATE A PHONY IMAGE—TRY TO EXPRESS REAL FEELINGS

It seems that we can become more valuable to society if we accept our inner feelings more readily.

Of course. I can give you a personal example. When I was raised, I did not learn how to develop close relationships with other people. I did not have a lot of friends when I was growing up, but I was always elected class president, because I would generally get the highest grades in the class. But I was an uptight and achieving type, and I certainly was not popular.

I remember, when I was in medical school at Stanford, I went to an encounter group because I thought that it was very intriguing. These were very much in vogue in the late '60s in California.

During this particular session, a woman described a dream, and the leader had her act it out and everyone discussed it. The whole procedure seemed harmless and entertaining. Suddenly, the atmosphere of the group changed, and after I offered my opinion, the people in the group confronted me and really put me down.

I believed that there was something about my behavior that they didn't like. I felt embarrassed and humiliated by their comments. At the end, most of the people in the group said that they had a wonderful experience, but I was just sitting there on the floor, with my head hanging down, feeling devastated by this experience. Then the director of the group came over and put his hand on my shoulder, saying, "Dave, what's wrong?" I told him that I was just feeling put down and kind of inadequate, like a loser. He said, "You know, when you are like this, quiet and subdued, I actually like you a lot more. You are always coming on so strong and trying to impress everybody—that really turns people off. When you're showing how you really feel inside, you become more likable." Up until that time, I had never considered what he was saying, but he planted a seed for me, and this insight grew over many, many years.

How?

We don't need to be the center of attention all the time; we can just accept our humanness. Feeling inadequate at times is part of it, feeling anxious at times is part of it, feeling lost or confused sometimes is part of it. But society leads us to believe that we've always got to be in control, we've always got to be confident, and we've got to make a lot of money fast, or we're losers. I believe that leading a life that is rich in emotions—positive and negative—is a very significant achievement.

WE CAN'T DEFEAT ANXIETY UNTIL WE SURRENDER TO IT

What else can people do—besides accepting their inner feelings—to overcome anxiety?

One of the most important keys to a successful therapy is this paradox: You can't defeat your anxiety until you surrender to it. You can't get rid of it until you embrace and accept it. That insight has many practical applications in therapy.

DEALING WITH ANXIETY: GET CONTROL OF STRESS AND BOOST SALES **197**

Are you saying that anxiety itself becomes part of the cure?
Yes. I remember one experience from high school. I had a fear of heights ever since I was little but wanted to be on the stage crew of the musical "Brigadoon" in my sophomore year. Being on the stage crew required climbing up at great heights above the stage. One day, the drama teacher asked me to stand on one of these tall ladders for about 15 minutes. I was terrified at first, but after about 5 or 10 minutes, the anxiety wore out and I wasn't nervous any more. After that experience I climbed all over the stage and loved it. My fear turned into euphoria. In medical school, I had the fear of blood.

That's the classic definition of a psychiatrist—a doctor who cannot stand the sight of blood. What did you do?
I got a job working in a clinical laboratory. My job was to stick needles into people's arms and draw blood. I decided to do the thing that I was afraid of doing. So I worked eight hours a day drawing blood and became one of the best in the Stanford Clinical Laboratory.

How did it go the first day on the job?
Once I decided to confront my fear, it only took about 5 or 10 minutes, and then I felt fine. It often does not take much exposure. Once you've made the decision, you've won half the battle.

ROLLED UP IN A RUG AT 2 A.M. IN THE BASEMENT

What is the probability of curing a phobia with this technique?
If you confront your fears that way, the probability of a cure is extremely high. If you don't confront your fears, the probability of a cure is very slim. When I tell that to my patients, they get very irritated, because they don't think that a simple approach could possibly help them. They want to lie on the couch and talk about it endlessly. The bottom line is either you confront your fears or you live with them forever.

I remember a top manager who had a fear of the dark and suffered from claustrophobia, the fear of tight spaces. One day while his wife was out of town for a fundraising event, I suggested that he confront his fears. I told him to set his alarm for two in the morning, go down to his basement with his flashlight, roll himself into the Oriental rug, and turn off the flashlight. I also told him to have a tape recorder ready and record his thoughts every 60 seconds during the experiment. At first he accused me of being irresponsible for suggesting this, because he was afraid that he would lose control and go crazy, but he agreed not to turn the lights on and not to run out of the basement, no matter how fearful he became. He got real anxious and had the fantasy that a fat ghost would sit on the rug and suffocate him, but after about 20 minutes, his nervousness went away, and the whole experiment became silly to him, and he became euphoric.

So, in a sense, allowing yourself to experience anxiety will become part of the cure.

We can't escape anxiety until we confront it, accept it, and surrender to it. Once we do that, the transformation is rapid. But it is not always so easy, because it is the last thing we want to do.

THE ACCEPTANCE PARADOX

Is the desire to run away closely connected to our feelings of anxiety?

Exactly. Once we decide not to run away, half the anxiety is gone. It's like saying to a bully, "Go ahead, take your best shot; I am not running from you!" Once you say that to yourself, with some degree of conviction and commitment, the anxiety loses its steam.

What if the anxiety comes back?

There are two principles to keep in mind. First, remember that your anxiety signals something is bothering you, so you've got to find out what it is.

The second is to accept the anxiety. Tell yourself it's perfectly normal and acceptable to feel anxious. You'll find that you continue to feel anxious for a while and then your symptoms will go away shortly. Part of the anxiety is the fear of anxiety. If I accept the anxious feelings, the anxiety will vanish, but if I fight the anxious feelings, the anxiety will increase. The anxious person fights even the slightest twinge of anxiousness. They say, "This is terrible! This is a serious case! I am going to go crazy! I am going to pass out! I am going to die!" They overdramatize and turn a minor drizzle into a major storm.

> *I imagine that anxiety is like a hurricane with powerful winds outside, and in the eye you reach a center of total calm.*

That's a good image. Once you've decided to move into the center of the storm, you'll discover a great feeling of peace.

THE FEAR OF PUBLIC SPEAKING

Have you ever experienced the fear of public speaking?
I enjoy speaking in public, and I have given lectures to groups of more than 1,700 people. But any time I have to present to a new type of audience, I get nervous. Recently I was asked to give a lecture on social anxiety at a Harvard-sponsored symposium at the Copley Plaza Hotel in Boston.

Hundreds of psychiatrists and psychologists attended. The ironic part is that fear of public speaking is a form of social anxiety. The speakers before me were luminaries, and my presentation was toward the end of the day. As I listened to superb presentations by these leading Harvard scholars, I asked myself, "What am I doing in a place like this? This is a major league event!" I found myself getting more and more nervous.

As I walked up to the podium, I was trembling and my mouth was dry, and I could barely muster the energy to speak and thought,

"I am supposed to show them how to treat social anxiety, and I can't overcome my own fear of speaking to this group!" It was absurd.

I began by saying, "One of the things I am going to discuss today is public speaking anxiety." I asked them, "How many of you have ever experienced public speaking anxiety?" About two-thirds of the hands went up, and many began to chuckle nervously.

Then I said, "That's exactly the way I am feeling right now." They all started laughing and were very accepting, and that broke the ice.

You made friends with the audience.
Yes, self-disclosure is one way to make friends quickly. Behind the fear of public speaking is the perception that people are going to be hostile. One of the antidotes is to befriend the audience. If you think the audience is full of hostile and uncaring individuals who are going to reject you, then you'll feel terrified, but once you've established a warm and personal relationship with your audience, you'll feel more confident and free of anxiety.

THE PROSPECTS FOR SUCCESSFUL TREATMENT

To what degree is anxiety curable?
The idea of a cure is an all-or-nothing thought. We should not aim for a life totally free of anxiety, but for living more fully and productively. The vast majority of people I treat improve dramatically after a short period of time using the techniques outlined in *The Feeling Good Handbook,* but some people with very severe and chronic problems will resist treatment, and it will require a longer period of time.

Why?
One reason may be a mistrust of the therapeutic relationship itself. Another is that some patients have had problems for 20 years or

more, and changing is sometimes alien and threatening. Sometimes it takes two years before they decide to bite the bullet and face their fears.

What do you suggest readers do to manage anxieties more effectively?

First, reread this chapter a few times to let the ideas grow and take root in their minds. Second, use *The Feeling Good Handbook*. The book is very action-oriented; it is really a self-learning guide that puts the critical skills into the hands of the reader. Third, talk to someone they are close to. When something in your life is bothering you, a compassionate relationship with another human being can be very helpful. It could be your spouse, a close friend, a rabbi, clergyman, or a professional therapist.

ACTION STEPS

ANXIETY

1. Awareness: Anxious people tend to deny their strong desires and feelings of anger or frustration. They are unaware that these hidden feelings cause anxiety.
2. Acceptance: Anxiety results in the failure to accept our humanness and our deeper feelings. We cannot escape anxiety until we accept it and surrender to it.
3. Action: Once we become aware of our repressed feelings, we need to take the appropriate course of action. This may involve being more open in the way we communicate with others or taking steps to solve personal and professional problems.
4. Attack your fears: The desire to run away is closely linked to the feelings of anxiety. Once you decide not to run, most of your anxiety will vanish.

Chapter 18

Dealing with Disappointment: The Disappointment Trap

Objective:

To help you understand the powerful forces involved in feelings of disappointment and ways you can use them to grow beyond your hidden, self-imposed handicaps.

Synopsis:

1. Disappointment is more than simply not getting what we want. Disappointment is what is created by the unconscious meaning we attach to these wants.
2. We should not be afraid to let our disappointment show. It does not mean failure and should not be viewed as such.
3. The best way to react to disappointment is to reflect on what has happened and move on.
4. Many people equate success and failure with being loved or not loved. This sets them up for disappointment whenever they stumble.
5. Disappointment is a growth factor. Without disappointment there can be no growth.

Dr. Abraham Zaleznik, the son of a Philadelphia produce market owner, studied the inner workings of the business world as a director of five companies, including the Ogden Corporation, Purity Supreme, and Pueblo International. Dr. Zaleznik, who holds a doctorate in commercial science, approaches the subject of disappointment from a very unique vantage point. He is, in fact, a certified clinical psychoanalyst, one of the few who make psychoanalytic thought and concepts accessible to business leaders and managers.

He taught at the Boston Psychoanalytic Society and at Harvard University Graduate School of Business Administration. Dr. Zaleznik is the Konosuke Matsushita Professor of Leadership Emeritus at Harvard University. From 1967 to 1983 he was the Cahners-Rabb Professor of Social Psychology of Management at Harvard Business School.

"Disappointment becomes a particularly significant experience," explains Dr. Zaleznik, referring to business executives, "because people don't know what to do." In the interview in this chapter, he referred to the suicide of Alan David Saxon in 1984, a Los Angeles gold dealer whose death had touched off a search for $60 million in precious metals presumed missing.

His concern for the individual in an organization is reflected in his penetrating books (*Power and the Corporate Mind, Orientation and Conflict in Career,* Harvard, 1975; *Human Dilemmas of Leadership,* Harper & Row), and many articles (see *Harvard Business Review,* "Managers and Leaders," May/June 1977 and "Management of Disappointment," Nov./Dec. 1967).

I met with Dr. Zaleznik in his Harvard University office, which was not only equipped with the proverbial psychoanalyst's couch but also with a computer linked to one at his home and another at his Florida "hideaway." This linkage suggested that he practiced what he preached as a first-line defense against disappointment: "Don't put all your eggs in one basket."

Dr. Zaleznik, you are a pioneer in researching the subject of disappointment. What does disappointment mean?
Dr. Zaleznik: Let's start with a superficial definition. You want something, you don't get it; the result is disappointment. But disappointment is not simply the result of not getting what one wants or expects. We need to examine what it is about that want that

grabs a psychological bite. What a person wants often has enormous unconscious value and, consequently, not getting it takes on a great deal of significance. The psychological event of disappointment may lead the individual to fall back on himself and discover that the world and his place in it has no meaning. One tragic example that made headlines would be the gold dealer in L.A. who killed himself. There has been a whole rash of suicides . . .

> *So you are saying that not getting what we want is not necessarily the key issue; it's the unconscious meaning we attach to those wants that creates the disappointment.*

Right. Let's say a person charges a business venture with certain unrealistic dreams. Not getting what he wants can lead to disappointment and so can getting what he wants. When a person finally gets what he has been working so hard for and sees that his unconscious dreams aren't realized, the result will be a tremendous disappointment. Take Henry Ford: His achievement of the Model T marked a turning point in his career. He became increasingly rigid and unrealistic in his thinking; he seemed to have experienced some disappointment in a fantasy attached to his achievement.

> *What are the most common misconceptions people have about disappointment?*

One, that it is bad. Two, there is a strong code in business that if we are disappointed, we are not supposed to show it.

> *Denial is encouraged.*

Yes, it is. If people show and react to their disappointment in public, they are going to hurt themselves. In a sense they are trapped if they don't know how to get help. Business is preoccupied with success. The world loves a winner; nobody likes a loser. So, people expect that they have to come on with a bright, cheerful, upbeat mask, because the world loves a winner. That's where I say it takes a great deal of courage. You have to be able to think, to experience what's going on, but at the same time recognize that nobody has a lot of sympathy.

> *So disappointment should not be viewed as negative, and it isn't equal to failure.*

No, it doesn't equal failure. Once it is seen in positive terms, I think people are then prepared to learn a great deal from the experience.

> *Do you think that the positive thinker prevents, avoids, or denies disappointment?*

There are various types of positive thinkers. There are some who have deep faith—like Dr. Norman Vincent Peale. I didn't know him personally, but I believe that he viewed that God had put him here to do something. That is a powerful belief that can sustain a person for a long time. He has a mission to accomplish in life, and there is no such thing as disappointment in the sense that the mission doesn't go away. Therefore, if you're lost, it simply means you haven't gotten there yet.

> *You said that there are different types of positive thinkers.*

There are some positive thinkers who think positive because it pays. There is a market for it. They have good marketing sense. They appeal to a wide range of fantasies. Positive thinking is part of the national character. If you don't like your job, you leave it and go elsewhere; if things don't work out there, you go someplace else. It is part of the American Dream.

There are also those in the field of self-improvement. They are different positive thinkers who say if you change the way you think about life and situations, it's going to get better and everything will work well.

Is that realistic?

It serves as a valuable myth for people who believe it. But it may not necessarily lead people to deal with the realities of whatever they are good at. The criticism I would have of certain positive thinkers is that they don't always understand that people have to develop disciplines and talents. Some are even holding out a false promise that it's easy: If I believe hard enough, I could become it. What nonsense! My friends in Austria have a word they use quite a lot: *Blödsinn*. What does that mean?

Idiocy.

It's used a lot in Vienna.

Are you saying that a positive thinker should spend more energy in developing the talents necessary to achieve?

Let's look at this issue from a different angle. I think the most tragic positive thinker of all time was Arthur Miller's Willy Loman in *The Death of a Salesman*. His character was a beautiful illustration of the idea that if you spend so much time attached to the dream and no time in figuring out what it is that you are capable of doing, you are bound to get disappointed. Instead of improving your talents, you are living with an illusion. That's my objection to positive thinkers. In life you need courage, but you don't need illusion.

Work Your Way out of the Disappointment Trap

Two Kinds Of Hurt   Disappointment can be separated into two major categories that range from global disappointments (the serious kind) to everyday disappointments.

1. A global disappointment has a tendency to become pathological. When people get depressed following a severe disappointment, they tend to become incapable of reexamining the conflicts and issues that have preceded the disappointment. They may produce certain chemicals in the brain that prevent them from (optimistically)

looking with clear eyes at anything. In these instances, professional help (psychiatrist, psychologist, mental health center) is essential.

2. Everyday disappointments are challenges for self-management and opportunities for personal growth. The every day disappointment is the counterpart of the gratification or frustration experience, necessary for development from childhood on.

Are you suffering from a minor disappointment? Congratulate yourself. It only means that you're growing. Constant gratification would be like living in a 100 percent sterile environment—totally unrealistic.

Establish New Priorities   Stop running. Think. Review your experience. If you are alone, put it on paper. If you have access to a good friend, talk it over. If the disappointment is related to your job, discuss it with your spouse first. Isolate minor disappointments before you see your next customer.

Minimize Your Exposure   One major source of disappointment: unrealistic expectations. We often overestimate what our abilities can do, what money can do, what authority can do, what contracts can do, and what other people will do for us. Disappointment in expectations helps us learn about the practical opportunities in life. Unrealistic self-expectations can lead to unnecessary disappointments. For example, Omar Bradley always considered himself a soldier; George Patton always considered himself a general. Patton could not live with anything less than total command of the situation, whereas Bradley served his Commander-in-Chief.

Increase Your Resistance   One key characteristic to lower your chances for suffering disappointment is to increase your ability to tolerate love and hate and avoid confusing them with indifference. How? Through commitment. Why? If your commitment to your job, your mission, or your goal is the global reason for deploying your energies, then love or hate do not become the personal reasons for doing something. For example: A deep commitment to customer satisfaction allows you to accept love and hate. In selling, some prospects will accept you, some will reject you, and some will just be indifferent. Your commitment will help you tolerate the different feelings that prospects have about you and the situation. It will help you understand that a rejection may be real or imagined.

Your deep commitment doesn't change the direction of your drives; it will help you move beyond love and hate. Commitments can transform the roadblocks of love and hate into clear pathways.

Put the Odds in Your Favor   Don't put all your eggs in one basket. Monitor your expectations. Know your abilities and limits.

Keep your eyes on your dreams. Renew your commitments every day. Accept other people's negative feelings and your vulnerability. Maintain conscious control over your drives. Build close relationships. Keep reaching higher. Get professional help when the hurt is alarmingly deep or someone close to you notices. Think.

The Bottom Line   Accept disappointments as growth experiences. Learn from them, or you'll sidestep growth by becoming cynical.

by Dr. Jack Schoenholtz

How would you define courage?

Courage is the willingness to look at life as it is, to look at yourself as you are, and to come to terms.

So you are saying it takes more courage to look at life as it is than to think positive?

Yes, because you don't need a screen to look at reality.

What are the most common reactions to disappointment? Are there certain stages people go through?

Many people get depressed, which is not entirely bad. There is also a predepressive reaction, a manic episode, in which people become hyperactive. It's a very dangerous time when they make rotten decisions and usually get themselves into trouble. They are better off getting depressed. To understand the true nature of depression, you have to understand rage. I won't say anger, because when there is a quantitative effect, it becomes rage. If you want to talk in terms of stages of disappointment, we would simply be looking at the transformations of rage.

Rage directed at . . .

Rage toward oneself for falling short. The enormous shame or humiliation that one has not measured up to the ego ideal [image of the ideal self]. Rage directed at others who didn't fulfill, rage at those who are withholding. I think that with all the openness in this society about sexuality, the big ugly secret is about rage. In this sense, disappointment becomes a particularly significant experience, because people don't know what to do. They are not familiar with the experience of anger or rage. They don't know how to simulate it and deal with it. In our society the emphasis is on teamwork, on getting along. So there is little room for dealing with disappointment.

How can we deal with it?
You can begin by accepting a kind of passive moment in connection with the disappointment. Withdraw from the battle. I don't mean to give up your job or family, but make a kind of psychological retreat. Allow yourself to deal with the experience. There are two ways people react to psychological difficulties: One kind of person tends to interact with others; the other kind begins to think. I think that the latter person has more going for him in the long run.

You are talking about introspection and self-examination.
I would guess that this is not the typical, everyday way of
dealing with disappointment.
No, it is not, because there are certain social pressures. People can't withdraw very well. But again, this is a very creative thing to know how to do. You have to have good fallback positions in which you're using your talents to reacquaint yourself or discover something new. Many great leaders have worked through their disappointments and emerged with greater strength. For example, Winston Churchill suffered great disappointment during World War I. He learned how to paint, he wrote, and he refocused his energies from the outer world to himself.

Do you see a way to prevent or reduce the risk of suffering
disappointment?
One sign of wisdom and maturity is to piece out one's ego investments. Unfortunately, very talented people often don't know how to piece things out and suffer catastrophic disappointment because they have put all their eggs in one basket.

*How about professional salespeople? How can they
minimize the risks of suffering disappointment?*

It's an interesting issue, because selling takes a curious combination
of desire and motivation, but it also takes a very realistic understanding of what you are selling, to whom and for what purpose.
You have to get that in a proper balance or one characteristic drives
out the other. One of the things that I judge to be very important
is not to mistake success and failure as being loved and not loved. If
salespeople personalize selling in these terms, then their self-esteem
is on the line. They set themselves up for disappointment. If I were
selling, I would try to get that under control.

What would you consider a good preventive measure?

I would develop expert knowledge about the product, the customer,
the market, and the competition. I would look at these facts realistically, examine the pluses and minuses, and then be prepared to sell
under those terms. I would not think of the sale just as the product
of a winning personality. On the other hand, I realize that you have
to have a lot of motivation to go out and sell.

How would you deal with a customer's disappointment?

Isn't this what makes a top salesperson? I would try to sort out
what the prospect expects from the product and deal with that
prior to the sale. Customers know that there are certain limitations
and need to understand what they are paying for. I think a good
salesperson tries to do a very good job examining what a prospect
needs to accomplish with the product. Also, experience will tell you
what people are looking for and what illusions they bring with
them. Effective selling takes a very good sense of how the world
works. It also takes self-knowledge.

Where would you put the emphasis?

On both.

This requires a lot of thinking . . .

Yes. One of the greatest virtues of the human mind is that you can think in relatively inexpensive terms. Action is always very expensive. Why not get the maximum mileage out of experience by thinking about it and doing less? The beauty of the human mind is that thinking is an experimental form of action—very inexpensive. There is no charge for thinking.

You've talked about Winston Churchill—how do you see
General Patton and how he handled disappointment?

Based on what I have read in biographies, I believe he never really came to terms with his fear about lack of manliness and courage. He became a superb field general reactively, because he was afraid of himself. One book documented that under moments of great stress and battlefield activity, he would take his pulse, and he would find it had accelerated and would be self-condemnatory. He was too hard on himself, but he also had difficulty understanding the nature of his fears. In that sense, he was vulnerable and susceptible to taking a lot of risks. As a commander, you have to remember that you must take care of your subordinates; otherwise, they will lose hope. The hope they have is that their authority figures have their best interests at heart and if they are sent on a dangerous mission, it's for the good of all. They don't do it to harm you. Commanders are calculating what is in the best interest of everybody.

How about your own disappointments—what was your
biggest disappointment?

When my father died, I was 20 years old and never had the chance to do with him what every young man wishes he could do with his father, which is to be close and to look at the world through his eyes for a while. That was the gravest of all disappointments for me. I got over it, but it took a very long time. That was a terrible experience.

You once wrote that preoccupation with success may be
less important than the role of disappointment in the
evolution of a career.

Yes. I believe that both the great strengths and weaknesses of gifted
leaders often hinge on how they manage disappointments—which
are inevitable in life. There are a number of studies and psychological biographies that support this conclusion.

Could you give us a few examples?

One would be Erik Erikson's psychological biography of Gandhi or
John Mack's study of Lawrence of Arabia. There are excellent
works analyzing leaders like Henry Ford, Frederick Taylor, John
Stuart Mill, and many more.

Based on these studies and your own experience, do you see
disappointment as a growth factor?

Yes.

Would you say that if you haven't had any disappoint-
ment, you haven't had any growth?

I would say that.

In which areas do you feel women manage disappointment
better or worse than men?

I think that they are more vulnerable by the social pressures that
restrict them from showing how they feel about things. In business,
if your heart is on your sleeve, you're going to get hurt badly. I
would think of this as a cultural problem. It's harder for them.

How do you separate your heart from your sleeve?

To cultivate a sense of separateness, to see oneself in terms of being
different. I don't mean being isolated, but being separate.

Separating the task from the person.

Yes, and getting a very clear understanding of what is going on
within oneself in the situation, so one's emotion can be dealt with.

*How about the role of drive and ambition in
disappointment?*

I think you could make an analogy with golf. The more ambitious you
are, the more difficulties you may experience with the game. Perhaps
the most effective people are those who modify ambition. Ambition is
different from drive. Drive is the desire for mastery, competence,
ability, and honing one's talents. Ambition is essentially a blind impulse.
Instead of trying to work at what you are doing and be better at it, one
projects a lot of energy toward vague goals.

*Where does the healthy drive end and burning ambition
begin?*

The healthy drive ends when you can't tolerate waiting. Burning
ambition is filled with impatience. One is torn and restless. But for
some people, it's just a fact of life. I wouldn't try to change them;
that's the way they are. We always have to keep in mind that there is a
powerful engine in the human being that can lead to great achievement. People often ask, "If it's analyzed, what will happen?" My
response to that is nothing will happen, if there is real talent there.

*Let's assume that a person has real talent and works
himself to the top. Let's also assume that that person has no
unrealistic dreams connected to his goals. Do you feel that
this talented and ambitious person will be lonely at the top?*

This is a myth. It's not lonely at the top. Henry Kissinger once said
that power is the greatest aphrodisiac. I would say that power can
be very therapeutic, and I think that people at the top have the
greatest life. Don't feel sorry for them. Of course, there is envy, but
that's very small compared to the riches one can enjoy in a position
of accomplishment.

ACTION STEPS

DISAPPOINTMENT

1. Isolate minor disappointments before they grow and affect other aspects of your life.
2. Minimize your exposure. Do not put all your eggs into one basket. Establish realistic expectations that allow for growth but don't drive you too far back when you fall short.
3. Increase your resistance. Commit yourself entirely to your goals, and any disappointments will be mere stepping stones to success.
4. Rediscover your true self. Learn and grow from disappointments. Don't sidestep growth by becoming cynical. Cynicism is the scar tissue of unresolved disappointment.
5. When the hurt is alarmingly deep, or someone close to you notices, get professional help.

Chapter 19

Dealing with Helplessness: How to Manage Your Negative Feelings

Objective:

To overcome the feelings of helplessness and insecurity that can plague salespeople, often creating selling inertia in even the most promising achievers.

Synopsis:

1. Feelings of helplessness can stem from both positive and negative experiences.
2. People who respond to a lost sale by thinking, "I am no good at this job; I can't sell this product," are courting passivity and helplessness.
3. The fear of failure often becomes a self-fulfilling prophecy.
4. Insecurities are the result of "guiding fictions," mistaken beliefs we hold as true that deprive us of our ability to cope with adversity.
5. Successful living comes only when we replace destructive guiding fictions with constructive positive notions.

When a prospect says "No," the salesperson's response—both immediate and long range—foretells a future of coping or quitting. If, after the immediate anger and frustration wear off, the salesperson is left with a residue of unresolved negative feelings about his or her ability to sell, then it's time to examine coping mechanisms. Perhaps it's also time to look at the salesperson's feelings of helplessness.

This exclusive interview with Dr. Martin Seligman, professor of psychology, University of Pennsylvania, shows how to get off the mental path that leads to helplessness and get on the road to quick recovery from the inevitable setbacks associated with selling.

What made you decide to study the subject of helplessness?
Dr. Seligman: Well, it was fairly early on when I was 13. I had just been sent off to a military school when my father had a series of strokes at age 49. He was entirely helpless for the rest of his life. I think that may have set the interest, and it was consolidated when I began my research at the University of Pennsylvania as a graduate student.

How do you see the role of helplessness in our lives in general?
I believe that the basic facts of life are that we are helpless in the great issues like birth and death. However, there is a window of control that we can either choose to open wider or let slam shut.

And you obviously found many new ways for opening that window.
I know the window can be opened much wider than people normally think.

How would you define helplessness for the layperson?
It is a response to situations where events are uncontrolled.

So the opposite of helplessness would be mastery, or control.
Yes.

So, according to your definition, positive events can also produce helplessness. Correct?
Absolutely. If positive events come to you independent of anything you do, then you get the same kind of helplessness induced by negative events. We call it "Success Depression."

Have you ever experienced a success depression?
No. Just the reverse. My successes have come by diligent effort and hard work.

*Can you illustrate the internal process of helplessness in a
selling situation?*
Let's take some negative, uncontrollable event like losing an important sale. You may perceive that you are helpless, you are lost, you are defeated. Then you ask what caused it. At this point in the flow of events, you can escape mental pain by saying, "My customer doesn't need this now," and that will take care of it.

You are opening the window.
Right. However, the poor salesperson closes it by saying, "I am no good at this job. I can't sell this product." If you interpret it that way, then you become passive, you tend to give up with a large number of customers, and you tend to blame yourself and feel bad about yourself.

*I have read your scientific study of life insurance
salespeople, and I would like to go through a quick
checklist of the consequences of helplessness. First, it saps
motivation to respond in future situations.*
Correct.

It disrupts the ability to learn from the situation.
I would add that it also inhibits the ability to be creative in the situation.

It lowers the expectation for future successes.
Right.

It produces emotional disturbances.
Specifically sadness, anxiety, and hostility. It also generates fear and depression.

It reduces the body's immune system.
Right.

And you found that salespeople earn less and their job
security decreases.

Both correct.

The big question is, What can we do about it? How do we
respond to tough situations in a confident, optimistic way?
How do we unlearn the helplessness response?

The president of Metropolitan Life asked me the same question.
We began our research by developing a questionnaire to predict
who was going to react this way. As a result, we immediately
lowered turnover by hiring people with what we call "positive
explanatory styles." Next, we developed a training program we call
"Optimism Sales Training." Essentially we introduce people to a
process for changing their explanatory styles. It is a four-day
program where people learn how to deal with overwhelming
negative thoughts. They learn to be more active and creative in the
face of failure.

Do you feel that there is a relationship between the way
we explain success and failure and our future sales
productivity?

I think the relationship is pretty direct. 1 think that those salespeople
who have adopted an optimistic style for dealing with negative events
will make the next call faster, they are going to be more creative on
the next call, and they are going to sell more.

They learn to recover more quickly.

Yes. Selling is a very special profession. We have tested many
different groups, from West Point students to Olympic athletes.
Selling is unique simply because you are exposed to the word "no"
a lot. Therefore, only a very special group of people is going to do
well in it.

*Do you feel that salespeople handicap themselves
more through making a mistake, or more through the
irrational explanation following the mistake?*
I think it is the explanation.

Have you ever been out on actual sales calls?
Yes. When my father had his stroke, I spent the next five years
selling magazines in upstate New York. At age 16, I was making
more money than I did until I was a full professor. I think there are
two aspects to selling. The first are the technical mistakes, and your
common sales training courses can help you with that. But your
training, your experience, and your talent can only go so far. Where
do you learn to think about the causes of your mistakes? That's a
second, special kind of skill. It is a learnable skill which most people
in selling don't have.

*So you are saying that if you learn that skill, you can
increase your sales further.*
Yes.

*Do you feel that the skill of explaining failure ultimately
determines our chances for achieving success?*
It puts the upper limit on your talent and ability. You can have
the talent of Mozart, but if you believe that you are no good at
composing music, you are not going to do anything.

*What is the difference between positive thinking and
learned optimism?*
There are two basic differences. When I think of your usual positive thinking or motivational speech, I think of it as a temporary
pumping up. It gives you a boost, but you don't internalize things.
You have to come back for another injection. The cognitive therapy techniques involved in learning optimistic explanatory styles
represent a new set of skills. They stay with you all the time.

Dan Oran, the president of your sales selection and train-
ing company, Foresight Inc., said that positive thinking is
statement-based, while cognitive therapy is question-based.

That's a fair assessment. There has been a lot of research to document the effectiveness of cognitive therapy. For instance, in the
treatment of depression, medication works about 70 to 80 percent
of the time. It works pretty well as long as you keep taking it. Once
you are off, you run as much risk of relapse as if you never had it.
You are going to get depressed again. Cognitive therapy has about
the same effect in relieving depression, but once you learn the
techniques, you acquire a skill for dealing with failure, defeat, and
mistakes that you will always carry with you. So when you get
defeated again, you don't have to run off to a doctor to get
pumped up again. The basic question you need to ask yourself is,
Do I want a temporary or a permanent solution?

Your research shows that our expectations determine our
level of success. What contributes to the development of our
expectations?

I think that there are two basic constraints on our expectations. The
main one is reality. And reality can be either pretty grim or pretty
bright. Then, on top of that, we've got our explanatory style. In
other words, the way we explain an event from the inside determines
our expectations. Reality is what constrains us from the outside.

You are a scientist, and you measure things a little bit
more carefully than the average person. What is your
measure of success?

For me there are two kinds of successes that really matter. One is
the "changing the world" success; the other is finding gratifying
successes in everyday life—the small challenges. I have to admit
that it appeals to me that you need to be doing something to make
the world a better place than the world you entered.

ACTION STEPS

HELPLESSNESS

1. A positive approach to negative events is a learned skill, not a trait. First, you must change your explanatory style of facing negative events.
2. Instead of blindly thinking positive thoughts, try to internalize the optimistic approach to negative events.
3. Before a sales call, actively visualize yourself presenting with confidence as you handle the customers' questions and objections.
4. During the call, use visual reminders for yourself, let silence work for you, and plan intermissions.
5. After the call, review the experience to continue to improve on your performance. No matter what happens, accept yourself for who you are.

Chapter 20

Plateauing: Overcoming Burnout and Complacentcy

Objective:

To avoid or prevent the sales phenomenon known as "plateauing," which affects salespeople who, although successful in the past, have since leveled off in their achievement.

Synopsis:

1. The plateauing syndrome may affect between 15 and 25 percent of all salespeople.
2. Symptoms of a plateaued salesperson include lackadaisical attitude toward paperwork, below-average working hours, lack of interest in or enthusiasm for new ideas, inappropriate use of business time and facilities, and, most important, flat sales.
3. The plateauing complex stems from a lack of motivation.
4. Plateaued sales reps have the potential to infect a whole sales force with their attitude.

Mike, 38, made over $180,000 a year in commissions from high tech surgical equipment sales and has just paid off his last bank loan. Now he spends Tuesdays at the country club and only works 30 hours a week. Janet, 27, meets her company's quotas every year, but lately she's become preoccupied with sifting through catalogues for graduate courses in business. She feels that her sales career is going nowhere. Joe, a 61-year-old life insurance agent, has only four more years before he retires. He doesn't come to work before 11 a.m. and engages in lengthy conversations about his woodworking to an exasperated office staff.

These three sales reps have plateaued, and they're not alone. According to a survey of 300 U.S. companies by the outstanding training firm Porter Henry & Co. Inc., executives see the problem all too frequently. Almost half of the respondents believe that 15–25 percent of their employees have stopped growing.

Porter Henry has shared the results of their study "The Plateaued Sales Rep" to help our readers and their companies recognize the early warning signs of "peaking out," eliminate the reasons for this plateau phenomenon, and take steps to motivate complacent salespeople.

These are problems that can be corrected, even prevented, once the first hurdle—recognizing that plateaued salespeople exist—is overcome.

TIPS

5 TIPS FOR MOVING BEYOND THE PLATEAU

1 Continually set and update goals for yourself as you progress and achieve. Here are my top three goals for this year:

_____

_____

_____

2 To be most effective, goals should be measurable, achievable, written down, deadlined, flexible, and consistent with your personal

TIPS

objectives. Here is how I will measure my top three goals:

_____

_____

_____

3 To achieve your goals, you must remain organized, delegate responsibility well, make time-conscious decisions, and address top priorities first. Here is how I am going to organize myself so I will reach my top three goals:

_____

_____

_____

4 The five top barriers to achievement are:
- Taking on too much at once.
- Getting bogged down in paperwork and red tape.
- Unforeseen crises—with proper "contingency planning," you can minimize the damage of unanticipated future events.
- Telephone interruptions—if you waste 30 minutes of phone time a day, that's the equivalent of 125 hours per year, or three whole weeks!
- Personal disorganization.

5 Three characteristics help Superachievers continue on their winning ways:
- Positive attitude—Winners focus on the positive inherent in all situations instead of letting life's inevitable failures discourage them from trying again.

> - Positive action—Winners are proactive in their approach to business. This high level of initiative, coupled with everyone else's inertia, make them successful.
> - Positive control—Winners accept accountability for the past and responsibility for the future. They pay little heed to naysayers, confident that they alone are responsible for their success or failure.

TELLTALE SIGNS

Patterns that can give managers clues to recognizing a potential plateau victim often go unnoticed. Over and over again, surveyed first-line sales managers and vice presidents alike said that their companies refuse to admit that the problem even exists. They label it a "temporary slump" or blame it on the employees' "poor attitude." However, once they acknowledge the plateau phenomenon, the warning signs are loud and clear.

- **Routine paper work:** Missed or ignored deadlines, incomplete forms, redundant or mechanical reports.
- **Working hours:** Long lunches, frequent absences, late starting and early quitting times.
- **Lack of interest:** Little or no participation at sales meetings, inability to solve sales problems, no enthusiasm for introducing new products.
- **Inappropriate use of time:** More time spent in the office than on calls, use of office equipment (copiers, phones) for personal projects (Little League, vacation plans).
- **Performance:** Marked drop or flat sales (a steady level with little or no change), little or no prospecting activity, increased customer complaints.

When salespeople exhibit these signs, it's time to find out why they have plateaued.

A COMMON PROBLEM

Many executives feel that up to a quarter of their sales force has leveled out. What's worse is that 6 percent of those surveyed set the figure even higher—between 40 and 75 percent! Why do so many reps plateau? Four of the most frequent explanations include:

- Enough income to meet needs and desires
- Dead-end positions
- Boredom
- Job burnout

They all boil down to a lack of motivation. Remember Mile? With commissions of over $180,000 a year, he'd rather relax and take time to spend money than expend energy to make more of it. Janet's company hires outside people for management. Because her avenues for promotion are blocked, she has the choice of becoming an overqualified salesperson, looking for a new job, or changing careers. Boredom strikes young employees who expect fast promotions and constant challenges and don't get them. Joe's lack of recognition at work might be the reason he's so enthusisastic about his hobby. Salespeople who pressure themselves to outperform everyone find that the price of sustaining that degree of energy and drive is high and can add up to mental and emotional exhaustion. Burnout victims eventually plateau, even if it's at a slightly higher level than their "average" coworkers.

When does the plateau phenomenon occur? All ages are susceptible, but it is most common in two groups: 45- to 50-year-olds and 25- to 30-year-olds. Whether they're sales veterans or fresh out of college, employees who aren't rewarded for their initiative simply stop trying.

THE SOLUTIONS

The savvy manger will first determine through observation and direct questioning why a salesperson has "peaked out." The next step is to try some, or all, of the following solutions.

REMOTIVATING FOR GROWTH

A three-pronged approach enlists the help of the company, the manager, and the individual salesperson:

The Company's Part

Salespeople are a valuable company resource. They are also human and need recognition for their contributions. Form "senior sales rep" clubs and award "master" jackets to older reps. Younger salespeople need to feel important. Fill them in on the goals and long-range plans of the company and ask for their input. Bonuses, incentives, and sales contents—compensation tied to performance—help to motivate the sluggish reps. Companies can also develop formal career paths and provide career counseling.

Management's Input

New assignments and leadership roles go a long way toward helping to solve the "peaked out" problem. Set higher goals for your salespeople—either sales goals or personal ones. Learning a new skill or opening a new account increases motivation. Probation, a choice well down on the list of suggestions, does more harm than good, especially for older salespeople. As one respondent noted, "Putting the older rep on probation is just going to drive him deeper into his hole. And when word gets around to the younger reps, it can really make the manager look like a heartless fool."

Other suggestions include district sales contests, monthly news and sales letters, new or review training, weekly sales meeting run by reps themselves, sales seminars, putting plateaued reps in charge of training new salespeople, and discussing the problem to work out solutions.

The Salesperson's Responsibility

Salespeople can't be helped until they're ready. They must recognize their problem and want to solve it. Once reps are willing to try, they can boost their skills and momentum by attending outside sales seminars, reading more professional books, periodicals, and newsletters, and getting involved in sales clubs or associations. Younger reps should reevaluate their career goals. Finally, all salespeople should create 2-, 5-, and 10-year plans for personal and professional growth.

TAKING PREVENTIVE ACTION

The easiest way to deal with the plateau phenomenon is to avoid it. Recognize that challenges and rewards are prime motivators. If you treat your reps like professionals, they'll do their best to meet your expectations. Encourage more communication by asking for salespeople's ideas about new selling strategies, training programs, or company policies. One manager suggested that several mini-reviews between annual evaluations help to locate potential problems early enough to head them off. When you communicate your interest in the rep through praise and advice, reps are more likely to bring their problems to management instead of waiting for a confrontation.

A company's most valuable resource is its people. Take your company from "peaked out" to peak sales by acknowledging the problem of plateaued reps. Then give them the incentive to start growing again.

ACTION STEPS

PLATEAUING

1. Take a leadership role in finding the keys to motivating yourself and your salespeople.
2. Take preventative measures by rewarding, encouraging, and training salespeople to achieve the best results, and then challenge them to surpass those limits.
3. If you want to move beyond the plateau, the solution lies in exerting positive control over your life, setting valid goals, and taking positive action.
4. Accept the responsibility for your future. Remember that nobody will ever have more confidence in your future success than you.

Chapter 21

Overcoming Procrastination: Get into the "Do It Now" Habit Starting Today

Objective:

To help you outsmart your procrastination habits, one of the most insidious problems many sales-people face.

Synopsis:

1. Although it may give us a temporary respite from stress, procrastination in the long run creates more stress and anxiety than it alleviates.

2. People procrastinate either because they are afraid of what might happen if they act or because they do not want to do anything that does not offer immediate pleasure.

3. When we procrastinate, we mistakenly think we won't have to suffer through the negative feelings associated with an unpleasant task. In reality, however, the task itself is neither pleasant nor unpleasant. It is our negative thoughts associated with the task that we fear.

Although procrastination never pays, many of us delay working on important tasks. Why? Because negative emotions like fear, anger, or anxiety interfere with our capacity to succeed. While brilliant logic produces the most elaborate plans, negative emotions can suspend them indefinitely. Dr. Dominic DiMattia, a psychotherapist and the director of corporate services at the Institute for Rational

Emotive Therapy in New York, has conducted hundreds of workshops for executives who want to kick the procrastination habit. His work has received worldwide recognition. In this exclusive interview, he shares his tested techniques for helping salespeople, sales managers, and customers overcome procrastination and boost productivity.

Why do people procrastinate?
Dr. DiMattia: People avoid doing things either because they fear that they won't do a good enough job or because of low frustration tolerance.

Let's take a sales manager looking at his plan for the first quarter of this year. Let's assume that the plan needs to be rewritten because several competitors have changed their pricing strategies. What would cause a sales manager to procrastinate in this case?

The most probable cause would be fear—the fear of the unknown or the fear of failure. Another reason would be what we call discomfort anxiety, or low frustration tolerance. The sales manager may not want to engage in an activity that does not offer immediate pleasure.

And not doing the plan means avoiding pain.
Yes. Rewriting a plan means that you have to sit at your desk and go over lots of material and collect new information. It is a solitary activity, and there is no immediate benefit associated with that type of work. Sales managers are very socially oriented and don't like working alone. And there is no immediate punishment for not doing it.

So there's no immediate punishment and no immediate gratification.
Yes. We all want to do something that brings us pleasure immediately. That's why rewriting this plan will appear as a real struggle. We don't like to force ourselves to think about a lot of problems. Also, the job involves dealing with uncertainty. We may think,

"Will I make it this year?" Or, "What if I don't make it?" Every job involves a certain amount of self-talk. We may catastrophize and say, "It will be terrible if I don't make it. What a horrible situation!" All of that is going to make us feel very uncomfortable. That's why we procrastinate.

Is that the reason why we fool ourselves into thinking that by not doing the job we'll instantly feel better?

Yes, but that's not all. We foolishly think that doing the report is what causes us to experience these negative feelings. We might say, "Well, if I didn't have to do this report, I would not feel any of this discomfort." In reality, we know that doing a report is neither pleasant nor unpleasant. What causes us to feel bad are our erroneous beliefs and thoughts associated with doing the report.

How can we avoid procrastination, become more efficient, and handle these unpleasant jobs without self-sabotaging delays?

The first step would be to take a quick break to identify and describe our emotional response to the job we are trying to avoid. Most people are completely unaware of their feelings of anger, anxiety, sadness, or depression related to their work simply because they have developed a whole range of avoidance behaviors.

Do you suggest taking a break, so we can look behind our defenses?

Exactly. You want to examine your thoughts and feelings. How? By asking yourself, "What am I thinking? What am I feeling right now? How does my body respond to this situation? What amount of pressure do I experience? Are my teeth clenched? Is my stomach in knots? Am I berating myself?" We could call this a Rational Effectiveness Break, where we sit down and scan our thoughts, feelings, and physical responses in relation to the job to be done.

Would we write this down on paper?
That can be very useful, especially for people who pretend that there is no place for emotional responses in the world of business.

What would be the next step?
Our objective would be to pinpoint the key emotions. Do I feel fearful? Do I predict that something terrible is going to happen? Fear almost always has a future orientation. Let's say we are revising our first quarter forecast. What will happen if we don't make these numbers? Or, do we feel angry? Anger always has a demanding quality. The operative words are "should," "must," or "have." Anger is often a reflection of a rigid and demanding attitude. We may say, "I should not have to do this report" or, "My salespeople should turn in their projections sooner so I don't have to bug them about it."

Another scenario would be that I feel guilty. I could say to myself, "I am not a very good manager. I should have stayed in sales. I don't do well when it comes to paperwork." Guilt is often caused by unrealistically high standards we impose on ourselves.

What you are saying is that our own thoughts are the major cause of fear, anger, and guilt.
Exactly. We need to accept the fact that our emotions are the result of our thoughts. We ultimately have to take ownership for our own ideas and stop blaming external forces for the way we feel.

How do we change the way we feel?
By changing our thoughts, we can begin changing our feelings. That's why we need to examine our thoughts objectively and look for irrational ideas. I am not saying that all of our thinking is irrational. Some of it is, and some of it isn't. We are all capable of producing subtle, self-defeating thoughts. We want to find the catastrophizing thoughts or exaggerations. We want to isolate unrealistic demands we make on ourselves that usually begin with "I should" or "I must." Once we find out what part of our thinking is

distorted or twisted, we can begin editing these thoughts and put them into more realistic terms.

How?

One way of doing that is to write your thoughts on the left side of a sheet of paper and then ask yourself some basic questions like: What are the facts? What would really happen if I did not make the numbers? How terrible would it really be? Has every sales manager reached his numbers every year? The answer is usually no. What usually happens to them? Well, they may have some difficulties, but nothing really terrible happens. Once you appraise these thoughts objectively, you will free your mind from these unrealistic and catastrophic thoughts. As a result, the task will become more manageable.

You mentioned earlier that some people develop a number of mental avoidance games to put off tasks. Are there any mental games that get people to perform tasks immediately?

There are some behavioral techniques that can be very helpful. For example, divide the job into small segments. You make a

---

CHANGING SELF-DEFEATING BELIEFS OF SUCCESS

For example, a life insurance sales rep's belief system says: "My worth as a human being depends on selling $6 million of life insurance this year. If I don't sell that much, I can't feel happy and worthwhile."

To help evaluate this (erroneous) belief system, the sales rep could consider appraising the advantages and disadvantages of his beliefs as in the example illustrated below:

Advantages: "This belief system keeps me motivated, it helps me make more calls, it helps me reach my goals, it helps me make money, it gives me a purpose in life."

Disadvantages: "When I don't reach my goal, I get angry, upset, or depressed. This belief system also brings a great deal of doubt and worry about my capabilities. This belief system makes me ignore my needs for feeling good. This belief system makes me angry and upset each time I lose a sale; this makes me work too hard. This takes some of the fun out of my job and my personal life. This belief system creates the illusion that work is life's only satisfaction. There are many other activities that I enjoy."

Conclusion: "I don't have to connect my self-esteem to my performance. I can do a super job in selling life insurance and enjoy high self-esteem. My new belief system is: "My worth as a human being can't be earned or be given to me by others. My worth as a human being depends only on how warm and loving I am toward myself. I'll connect my self-esteem only to my need for feeling good. I'll give it to myself unconditionally. Thus, I'll reach my sales goal with less emotional strain and more self-satisfaction. Feeling good all the way!"

commitment to yourself that you will work only 20 minutes on the project. That's a manageable amount of discomfort.

Often the toughest part of a report is the beginning. You can create a small reward system for yourself to get you started like, "I will work on that report for 45 minutes, and then I will do something that brings me pleasure." Another behavioral technique would be to use self-affirmations like, "It is better to do things now than to put them off." Or, "I won't die from doing unpleasant jobs." Or, "Successful people fail more often than unsuccessful people." These affirmations can help you cope at work. In our seminars we hand out small reminder cards that people can put in their wallets.

How easy is it for people to learn these new habits for overcoming procrastination?

They are fairly easy to learn. However, as with any new learning, people tend to slip back to their old behaviors. The learning process is very similar to learning a new sport. If you want to play tennis well, you have to practice. If you want to become a "do-it-now person," you have to practice every single day. Old ideas will keep creeping back until you change your underlying beliefs. Once they have changed, it will become automatic.

Are there certain personality types that have a greater tendency to procrastinate than others?

In my opinion, they come in two categories. First, there are the perfectionists. The possibility of doing something in an inadequate way is very overwhelming to them. If they do something that turns out to be bad, they imagine that they are in real serious trouble. There is a second group of people that we could call spoiled brats. These are usually very bright people who tend to come from affluent families. They are intelligent and have well-polished social skills, but at the same time they have extraordinary expectations. They tend to act like prima donnas and refuse to do any of the unpleasant tasks. They are procrastinating because they are victims of their illusions of grandiosity.

If you are a sales manager and have a procrastinator on your sales staff, how would you deal with him or her?

The natural tendency is to get very frustrated and annoyed with these people. If you let your emotions take over, you are likely to engage in counterproductive behavior. So, the first step is learning to keep your cool.

> *Could we role-play a scenario? I have five salespeople. One*
> *of them, Larry, is getting me upset because I have to*
> *remind him every week to turn in his sales reports.*

Did you hear that? Larry is getting you upset. Larry has nothing to do with it. The real issue is that you are getting yourself upset by demanding that Larry be a more responsible individual. It is unrealistic to demand that all salespeople behave the way you think they ought to. That does not mean that you should leave Larry alone. What I am saying is that you need to change your internal dialogue first, so you don't get upset and you are free to deal with Larry's problem.

> *Are you saying that in order to help Larry, I have to make*
> *sure that I don't become part of his problem?*

Yes, you don't want to have a knee-jerk reaction to the situation, and you don't want to behave in the habitual way. It's not effective, yet you continue to do it.

> *I need to decontaminate my mind before I can talk to*
> *Larry?*

Yes, the key to managing other people is to manage our own emotions.

> *In other words, I need to scan my own thoughts and*
> *untwist them to dissolve any negative feelings.*

Yes. You want to condition yourself emotionally before you talk to Larry. That's very important. It's the key to effective management. It is the foundation to learning, thinking, and decision making. Good decisions are only made when the negative emotions are gone.

> *But some managers expect everybody else to do the work*
> *and don't expect to be bothered with emotional problems*
> *like Larry's procrastination.*

That's about the most irrational idea managers can have. It is totally unrealistic to think that they should not be bothered with these kinds of problems. The only purpose for having a manager is to deal with these problems. If everybody did their jobs, there would be no reason to hire a manager.

Are you saying that emotional management is one of a manager's key jobs?

Yes.

But many of us don't do our job too well in this area.

Managers don't like unpleasant situations. They don't like people to be mad at them. They have a high need for approval. They don't want other people to say bad things about them. They don't want to nag their subordinates too much.

They also want an office climate that is emotionally sanitized.

Of course. Emotional littering isn't tolerated. Managers tend to suffer from discomfort anxiety. They do not like unpleasantness at all. They don't like people crying; they don't like people mad at them. They want everyone to be sweet, nice, and lovely.

Let's go back to our role play. Can I ask you to play the sales manager while I play Larry?

"OK. Larry, there are several reports that are way overdue. I know that they may not be the most enjoyable activity in the world, but whether you like it or not, these reports have to come in. I really need to know what's keeping you from doing this."

"I was too busy last week. You wanted me to go after those new accounts. You want new business, and I am bringing you the new business. Nobody else is. Look at my sales record. I am the top salesman of the month. I can't do any more than I do now. I don't see how I can get you these reports and keep you happy with new sales."

"Well, that's unfortunate. It really is. But that doesn't change the reality. These reports have to be in. How can I help you get these reports in on time?"

"I don't have a secretary. Perhaps you can have your secretary do my reports."

"Well, we might be able to get you some more help to type these reports, but you still have to give us the data. You have to sit down and produce the numbers, even if somebody else types it up. What's keeping you from doing it?"

"I don't have the time."

"OK, let's look at that more clearly. Give me a complete, detailed outline of every day this past week. I want to know exactly what you do."

"I start at seven in the morning and make calls until seven at night. I call on about 12 prospects a day."

"And there are no moments in the day when you are not working?"

"Unfortunately, none."

"Well, if this is really a problem for you, perhaps I need to travel with you for a few days. Perhaps I can help you find periods of time when you might be able to put these reports together. It sounds like you are overwhelmed and you really can't handle what is required. Perhaps your territory is too big. But I really want to make it very clear to you that we have to come up with a solution to this problem. We have to get the reports in on time. And if it really requires you to do them on weekends, I'm afraid that's what is going to happen."

"OK, thanks."

What do you think I was doing?

> *Well, from an attitude point of view you were firm and*
> *understanding at the same time.*

What do you think my focus was?

> *You focused on getting my report.*

Yes, that's true, but I never got off the real issue. No matter what excuse you threw at me, I didn't get into an argument with you. I never called you a liar. I never said you could not do it. I just kept saying that the report must be done.

The report must be done. That's the key. It's the persistent focus on your behavior. I am not going to be intimidated by the best salesman of the month; I am not getting upset because you're saying that you don't get enough help; I am not getting mad at you for trying to weasel out of your job. The bottom line is that it is your responsibility.

What if you had a really obstinate salesperson?
I would set up a contingency. I would say, "Well, let me see if I can help you. The fact is that if you don't get the report in, we are going to delay your reimbursement until the report is in. That's just the way it has to be."

What if the salesman gets angry?
I would say, "You can get yourself worked up about this, or you can learn to accept some of the things that you don't like. Why are you getting so angry at me because I am insisting that something has to be done?" A good sales manager would also try to teach these techniques to the entire staff.

How about dealing with a customer's tendency to procrastinate? Do the same techniques apply?
The first step is to stop demanding that the client give you an answer right now. Accept the fact that some clients are slow to make decisions. Avoid putting too much pressure on yourself. Let's say that your sales are down and you sense that your client is procrastinating on making a decision. If you are getting yourself worked up about it, you're not going to make the sale. If you tell yourself, "I've got to get him to sign right now," then you're likely to increase your customer's fears and blow your chances of making the sale. Whenever we get nervous about something we want, we start overkilling and prevent ourselves from getting what we want. It's a self-sabotaging behavior.

So we need to condition ourselves emotionally prior to calling on the client.
That's right.

*Can we role-play a situation where you assume the role of
the salesman?*

OK.

"I don't think this is a good time for buying your seminar. I
don't know what is going to happen with this economy!"

"Well, let's take a look at what your needs are right now in your
business. You and I both know that the economy is not very stable
and chances are that it will continue to be unstable. How do you
see your needs?"

"We do have some needs, but I'd have to think about this some
more."

"I understand. Let me help you work through some of these
issues right now. You told me earlier that you had several salespeople who are not functioning well. If you delayed this training,
what would be the outcome?"

"I am not sure that your training is really going to improve the
bottom line."

"Tell me what you like about our training—the qualities that
make it different from the others."

"I think it's more reality-based. It creates better attitudes in people. And you have very good references. But my problem is that my
boss is really very nervous about investing $12,000 in this reces-
sionary market."

"Well, what would happen if you invested $12,000 in this
program and your sales did not improve as a result of this training?"

"Well, my job would be on the line."

"So let's assume you don't do the training and you save the
$12,000 in the short term. What will happen to your sales and
profits when the behavior of your salespeople continues to deterio-
rate? What will it cost you during the next three quarters?"

"I don't know."

"It could be pretty devastating. You know, it sounds as if you're
trying to apply a Band-Aid solution to a surgery problem. Your

solution may sabotage you in the long run. It seems to me that there is a greater risk and higher cost in leaving things the way they are. In order for you to be sure that this training is going to solve your problem, we need to sit down and customize the program. This way we can stop the erosion in your sales and also increase your profitability. I think that you want to plan your future by taking action, not to gamble it away by leaving things the way they are."

That sounds good. What if the customer tells you "No!"
I would shake your hand and say, "Thank you very much. I really appreciate the opportunity. If you change your mind, please give me a call. I'll get back to you soon." The key is not to get upset or angry. Just go back and try again. In other words, just be persistent. Keep at it and don't allow your emotions to get in the way.

> *Some salespeople think if they give the customer enough logical reasons for buying, the customer ought to make a decision.*

That's irrational. People have a right to think any way they want. If they want to think foolishly, let them. As a salesperson, you are operating with numbers. The more people you contact, the more you persevere—without alienating people—the greater the probability that you will close sales. The more you get demanding about closing a certain sale, the greater the probability that you will not only sabotage that sale but probably several others after that. It's classic behavior for salespeople to spend the afternoon in a movie theater or wandering around aimlessly, thinking about ideas instead of applying them. If you want to be successful, you have to keep working.

> *So, in conclusion, to overcome the procrastination within ourselves, with a salesperson or a customer, we need to create a neutral emotional climate. We need to prepare ourselves. We need to avoid getting angry, anxious,*

depressed, or guilty. We need to keep untwisting our
thinking and accept reality. Then we need to stay
focused on the key issues without alienating people.

That's exactly right. The larger issue here is that we need to work for long-term gratification. In other words, we can't expect to change a salesperson during one meeting, like we can't expect our customer to buy on the first call. We need to keep on building and building and building. Whether it's selling or managing, we need to be vigilant and persistent.

ACTION STEPS

PROCRASTINATION

1. When facing an "unpleasant" task, pinpoint the emotions that are causing you to put it off.
2. Write down your feelings to show you that the problems associated with the task are not catastrophic.
3. If the task is time-consuming, make deals with yourself to accomplish it in small segments.
4. With a procrastinator on your sales staff emphasize that certain tasks need to be completed, but don't attack your salesperson's character.
5. If you have customers who procrastinate, find out what their concerns are and how you can address them.

Chapter 22

Dealing with Stress: Eleven Steps to a Calmer You

Objective:

To give you simple, clear-cut methods for dealing with the daily stresses every salesperson faces. In addition, you will learn how to manage stress so it does not lead to the never-ending sales slump known as burnout.

Synopsis:

1. Stress is the result of dissatisfaction in one of four areas of life: physiological, sociological, psychological, or spiritual.
2. There are specific ways to help deal with both day-to-day and long-term stress.
3. Not all stress is bad. The difference lies in distinguishing between good stress (eustress) and bad stress (distress).
4. Whether you experience eustress or distress is determined by how you prepare yourself for change.
5. Burnout results when you can't cope with mounting stress and dissatisfaction in your life.

Stress is an inescapable part of modern life. But you can change the way you react to it. The following suggestions for stress reduction will help you relax and enjoy life. As a dividend, you'll be more productive, so you'll create less stress for yourself in the future.

1. **Laugh:** Laughter is one of the best tension releasers there is. Find things to laugh about and people to laugh with. Laughter is a great antidote for taking life too seriously.

2. **Take breaks:** Learning to interrupt a stress-producing activity will help give you the break from tension that you need. You'll return to your activity refreshed and ready to be more productive.

3. **Make "happy" plans:** Anticipation is an exciting feeling. Plan to see a special movie, eat out with someone you like, or do something else that pleases you.

4. **Focus your thoughts:** The habit of thinking about too many things at the same time is extremely fatiguing and stress-producing. Instead of being overwhelmed and unproductive, concentrate on one task at a time. Try making a list of other things you must do and then put it aside, so that you don't have to think about them, but you won't worry about forgetting them either.

5. **Check yourself:** Stop to see if you are relaxed. Are your hands clenched? Is your jaw tight? Such tension will begin to spread throughout your body, so catch it early. Let your arms hang loosely, unwrinkle your brow, relax your mouth, and breathe deeply.

Expert Advice: This chapter features contributions from **Pat Garnett**—Should be able to get something from Laura . . . he was the co-author for a SP book.

6. **Tackle the hardest jobs first:** This will give you a sense of tremendous accomplishment and provide momentum for finishing your other tasks. The pleasant things you must do will make your final hours at work enjoyable if saved until last.

7. **Go task by task:** If you finish one task at a time, you will avoid feeling fragmented and overburdened. It is also easier to see where you're going with a job when you give your full concentration. Leave some time between activities to minimize overlapping.

8. **Move:** Speed up your body action by moving to music, stretching, or taking a jog. Movement helps eliminate pent-up stress by aiding the removal of chemicals that stress produces that make you feel bad.

9. **Manage your time:** Use a plan of action. Schedule only as many tasks each day as you can reasonably finish without pressure. Leave time in your schedule for the unexpected.

10. **Help someone and smile:** Lending a helping hand or smiling can do what other methods of relaxation can't do. They give you a wonderful feeling of happiness and well-being.

11. **Enjoy yourself now:** Stop whatever you're doing and delight in being alive. Sense the physical processes inside you, the good in people around you, and the beauty of the world you live in.

DEALING WIHT STRESS **255**

TIPS

11 ADDITIONAL TIPS FOR COPING WITH STRESS

- Learn to say "no" to burdensome demands.
- View difficulties as challenges leading you to your goals.
- Understand that you cannot control everything.
- If you repeatedly fold under sudden stress, you may want to find a less stressful career.
- Don't be crushed if you fail.
- Rely on a solid group of family and friends to help you face stress.
- Keep it all in perspective. Your boss can't take away your life, family, or home.
- Find activities that help you relax.
- Exercise to help build your physical and stress stamina.
- Learn to use pressure to motivate and help you to achieve more.
- If you sense the symptoms of burnout, take stock of where you are and where you're going before it's too late.

ACTION STEPS

STRESS

1. Find out what aspects of your life are causing you to feel more stress than you can handle.
2. Prepare for stress and you will control it instead of the other way around.
3. Look upon future challenges as opportunities. Make strong choices guiding you in the direction you want to go.
4. Monitor your level of stress, manage your energy level to deal with it, and maintain a position of confidence and stability. This will help you avoid burnout.

Index

About the Author

© Hisham Bharoocha

A dual citizen of both Austria and the United States, Gerhard Gschwandtner is the founder and publisher of *Selling Power*, the leading magazine for sales professionals worldwide, with a circulation of 165,000 subscribers in 67 countries.

He began his career in his native Austria in the sales training and marketing departments of a large construction equipment company. In 1972 he moved to the United States to become the company's North American Sales Training Director, later moving into the position of Marketing Manager.

In 1977 he became an independent sales training consultant, and in 1979 he created an audiovisual sales training course called "The Languages of Selling." Marketed to sales managers at Fortune 500 companies, the course taught nonverbal communication in sales together with professional selling skills.

In 1981 Gerhard launched *Personal Selling Power*, a tabloid-format newsletter directed to sales managers. Over the years, the tabloid grew in subscriptions, size, and frequency; the name changed to *Selling Power*; and in magazine format it became the leader in the professional sales field. Every year *Selling Power* publishes the Selling Power 500, a listing of the largest sales forces in America. The company publishes books, sales training posters, and audio and video products for the professional sales market.

Gerhard Gschwandtner has become America's leading expert on selling and sales management. He conducts webinars for such companies as SAP, and *Selling Power* has recently launched a new conference division that sponsors and conducts by-invitation-only leadership conferences directed toward companies with high sales volume and large sales forces.

For more information on *Selling Power*, its products, and its services, please visit www.sellingpower.com.

Subscribe to *Selling Power* today and close more sales tomorrow!

GET 10 ISSUES – INCLUDING THE SALES MANAGER'S SOURCE BOOK.

In every issue of *Selling Power* magazine you'll find:

■ **A Sales Manager's Training Guide** with a one-hour sales training workshop complete with exercises and step-by-step instructions. Get a new guide in every issue! Created by proven industry experts who get $10,000 or more for a keynote speech or a training session.

■ **Best-practices reports** that show you how to win in today's tough market. Valuable tips and techniques for opening more doors and closing more sales.

■ **How-to stories** that help you speed up your sales cycle with innovative technology solutions, so you'll stay on the leading edge and avoid the "bleeding edge."

■ **Tested motivation ideas** so you and your team can remain focused, stay enthusiastic and prevail in the face of adversity.

Plus, you can sign up for five online SellingPower.com newsletters absolutely FREE.

FOR FASTEST SERVICE CALL 800-752-7355
TO SUBSCRIBE ONLINE GO TO WWW.SELLINGPOWER.COM

☐ **YES, I want a one-year subscription to *Selling Power* magazine.**
I will get 10 issues per year for only $27, that's 54% off the cover price.

Name: _____ Title: _____

Company: _____

Address: _____

City: _____ State: _____ Zip: _____ Phone: _____

☐ Check enclosed   Charge my ☐ Visa ☐ MC ☐ AMEX ☐ Discover

Card number: _____ Exp.: _____

Name on card: _____ Signature: _____

SellingPower.

For fastest service call 800-752-7355 • To subscribe online go to www.sellingpower.com

Open More Doors. Close More Sales.

Maximum Impact

ALSO AVAILABLE IN THE SELLING POWER LIBRARY

Great Thoughts to Sell By • The Psychology of Sales Success
Be In It to Win • Sales Stories to Sell By • Secrets of Superstar Sales Pros

SellingPower SellingPower SellingPower SellingPower SellingPower SellingPower SellingPower
SellingPower SellingPower SellingPower SellingPower SellingPower SellingPower SellingPower

for any Sales Career

McGraw-Hill books are available at special quantity discounts to use as premiums and sales promotions, or for use in corporate training programs. For more information please contact us at bulksales@mcgraw-hill.com, or contact your local bookstore.

Visit us at www.sellingpower.com/bookstore.   *Available everywhere books are sold.*